Fun Facts & Amazing Activities for Curious Kids

350+ brain-building
STEAM facts and exciting projects
to do at home!

SERGEI URBAN

*This book is dedicated to my sons,
Alex and Max, for always being
curious enough to ask "Why?"
and being patient enough to wait
while Dad Googled the answer.*

TABLE OF CONTENTS

8 Introduction

10 Giraffes Can't Swim
Biology, the natural world and real-life super-animals.

36 A Slice of Pi
Math, numbers and animals that can count.

54 It's Elemental
Chemistry, atoms and 2,000 helium balloons.

76 Out of This World
Space, physics and golf on the moon.

94 Totally Tectonic
Geoscience, culture and the rock we call home.

112 Careful, the Robot May Byte
Engineering, technology and flying cars.

132 That Never Gets Old
History, origins and Viking tweezers.

150 Look at That Van Go!
Art, yarn bombing and robot rock bands.

168 Afterword

INTRODUCTION

HEY THERE!

I'm Sergei Urban. You may know me as that guy from TheDadLab who turned his kitchen into a colorful battlefield of baking soda and vinegar. I'm no Nobel Prize winner—far from it—so, why am I writing a book about everything from the microscopic wonders of biology to the gargantuan mysteries of space?

EYES ON THE PRIZE!

Well, because I am incurably, irrepressibly, irresistibly curious. And there's a pretty good chance you are too!

If there's even a tiny spark of curiosity in you, this book will fan it into a bonfire of fascination. And who doesn't love a good bonfire?

If you're anything like me, you know that there's nothing better than the joy of discovering something new. For example, did you know that you are, at this very moment, hurtling through space at the speed of 66,000 mph? I know, wild, right?

But curiosity—and this book—isn't just about examining facts. It's about rolling up your sleeves and getting your hands dirty (sorry about that

Fun Facts & Amazing Activities for Curious Kids

in advance). And by dirty, I mean covered in squished blueberries, food coloring or even homemade red onion juice, because every chapter is paired with an exciting hands-on (and often messy) activity.

These experiments are the perfect excuse for some quality time with your family and friends, because shared moments of laughter, surprise and learning are priceless. But hey, if you're more of a lone ranger, that's fine too. You can still have a blast discovering and experimenting on your own.

So, are you ready to see just how incredible, strange and mind-boggling our universe is? Excellent! Let's get started. Enjoy the ride and don't be surprised if you feel your brain expanding at an alarming rate—it's just all that juicy knowledge settling in!

One more thing: As you read, you'll find red letters scattered throughout each chapter.
Write these down as you spot them—they will reveal a hidden message!

Giraffes Can't Swim

Biology, the natural world and real-life super-animals.

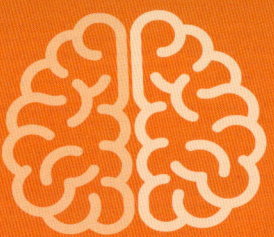

Your brain is divided into left and right sides, or hemispheres. Interestingly, the left side of your brain controls the right side of your body, and the right side of your brain controls the left side of your body!

When breathing through your nose, it may feel like you're breathing equally through both nostrils. Interestingly, this isn't the case—we only breathe through one nostril at a time, and often we breathe more frequently through one nostril than the other!

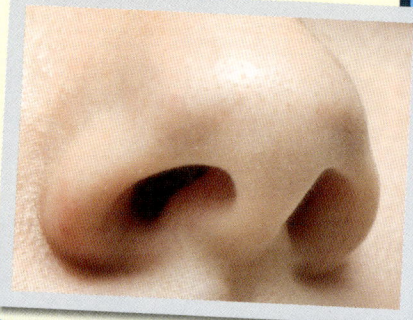

Ever wished you were just a little bit taller? Well, although it's hardly noticeable, you are about 0.4 inches taller when you wake up in the morning than you are when you go to sleep at night! During your sleeping hours, when you are lying down in a resting position, the cartilage (a soft and bendy material in your body that helps your bones move smoothly) in your spine doesn't have to support your body weight and spreads out, bringing about this slight change.

Did you know that your skin, the largest organ in the body (yes, it's an organ!), is actually very heavy? It accounts for approximately 15% of your total body weight! It's made up of three individual layers—the epidermis, the dermis and the hypodermis. Its thickness varies throughout the body, too. For example, the skin around your eyes and on your eyelids is the thinnest. It's thickest on your palms and the soles of your feet.

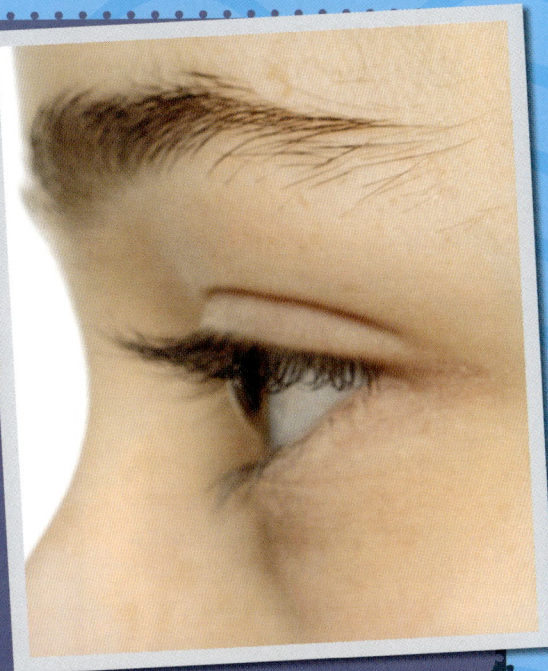

Every day, you take an average of 7,500 steps—that's about 3 miles. When you're 80 years old, if you've stuck to that amount every day, you'll have walked about 87,000 miles throughout your entire life! That's the equivalent of walking around the Earth at the equator approximately 3.5 times.

DNA is truly fascinating! Did you know that we share 98.8% of our human DNA with apes? But then, you might wonder, how did we turn out so different? Numbers can tell us a lot about these crucial differences and how they came about. You see, "base pairs" are important bits of information that determine the features of a living thing, and every cell in the human body has about 3 billion of these base pairs. Although only 1.2% of our base pairs are different than those of apes, that amounts to 35 million potential differences!

The functioning of the human body is dependent on a good night's sleep. Our abilities are damaged after missing even one or two nights of sleep, and going more than 10 days without sleep can be fatal! However, this is not the case for all life on Earth. Some birds that migrate only need a small amount of sleep over several months, and dolphins only sleep with one part of their brain at a time, meaning a part of their brain is always awake.

It's not only snakes, frogs and dogs that shed their skin—humans do it, too. Every 28 days, the entire surface of our skin is replaced—not all at once, of course! We shed each skin cell individually over this time. This means you'll have about 1,000 skins in your lifetime!

TEST THE SCIENCE NOW!

- Ever tried to lick your own elbow? If not, give it a try right now. It's impossible for most people to perform this seemingly simple task.

- It's also impossible to hum and swallow at the same time. Don't believe me? Give it a try right now! These two tasks cannot biologically be performed at the same time because when we hum, we are actually exhaling air. Because our airways close when we swallow to avoid the accidental inhalation of food, the air can't escape to create the humming noise.

- If you can roll your tongue into a tube shape, you're one step ahead of some others! Many people never develop this ability. Try it now and find out if you can.

- Surprisingly, only about 30–40% of the population can raise one eyebrow without raising the other. Can you do this?

- While it may feel like you lie awake in bed for a while before you drift into sleep, it actually takes only 7 minutes to fall asleep on average. Can you beat this time?

- How long is your tongue? Only around 34% of people are able to touch the tip of their nose or their chin with their tongue. Give this a try and see if you're one of them!

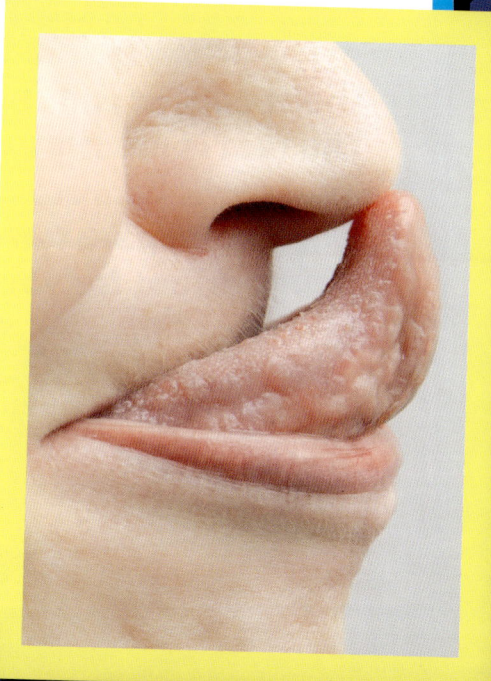

While we tend to think about mushrooms as plants, scientists who studied their family tree found that mushrooms (a type of fungi) are actually more closely related to animals than plants.

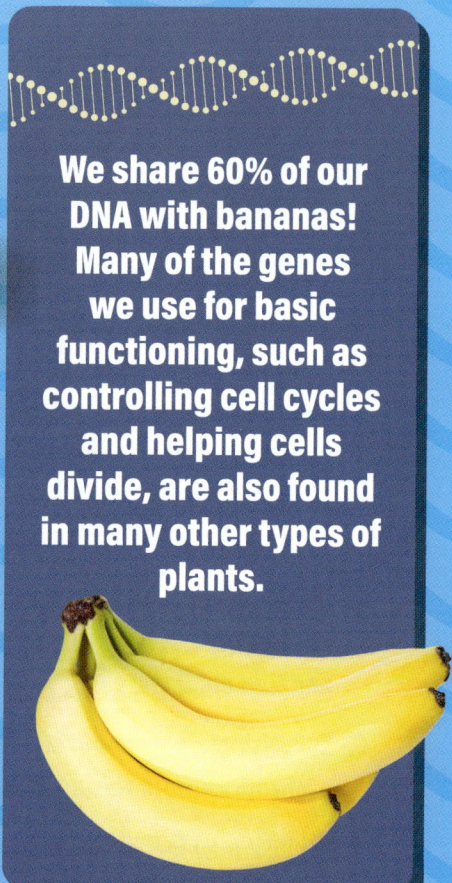

We share 60% of our DNA with bananas! Many of the genes we use for basic functioning, such as controlling cell cycles and helping cells divide, are also found in many other types of plants.

About 60% of your brain is made up of fat. The rest is mostly water, protein, sodium and carbohydrates. This means that an intake of omega-3 fatty acids is actually very important for your brain functions.

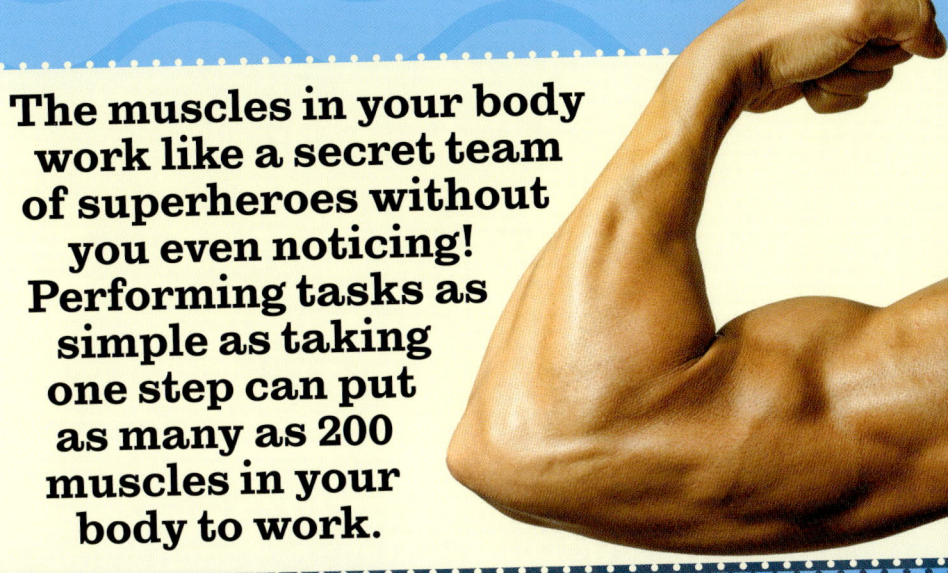

The muscles in your body work like a secret team of superheroes without you even noticing! Performing tasks as simple as taking one step can put as many as 200 muscles in your body to work.

Like skin, our taste buds are also renewed on a regular basis. A single taste bud only lasts for ten days before a new one takes its place! Burning your tongue by eating foods that are too hot can also speed up the life cycle of taste buds, prematurely killing them off.

In 2018, a new human organ was discovered! Yes, another one! It's called the interstitium, and it's a network of compartments throughout the body that are filled with fluid. It plays a role in tissue structure and our immune responses, and it may even affect how our bodies respond to potential threats.

Scientists sequence DNA to understand the genetic code that makes each living thing unique. DNA does not last long—about every 1,000 years it loses 75% of its genetic information. That is the reason we do not have dinosaurs' DNA. However, the oldest strain of DNA we've ever sequenced was taken from fossilized mammoth teeth left by mammoths that lived over a million years ago!

Did you know that you have more bones when you're a baby than when you're an adult? It's tr**u**e—babies are born with 300 bones, but by adulthood, we only have 206. This is because some of our baby bones fuse together over time.

Think bone is the hardest substance in your body? Think again! It's actually enamel—this is the substance that your teeth are made of. While this makes your teeth incredibly strong, regular brushing and dental appointments will ensure that this durable substance lasts a lifetime.

When you develop a scar after being wounded, you might notice that this scarred area doesn't grow any hair or produce sweat. This is because regular skin has lots of special cells that scar tissue can't regrow. It's also less resistant to sun damage.

Our bones might be heavy, but animals that fly can't afford all that extra weight. Budgies (short for budgerigars) are one such animal whose bones are, in fact, completely hollow, making them lighter, which makes flying easier. Some hollow bones are filled with air sacs that are connected to the bird's lungs. This structure helps birds take in more oxygen during flight.

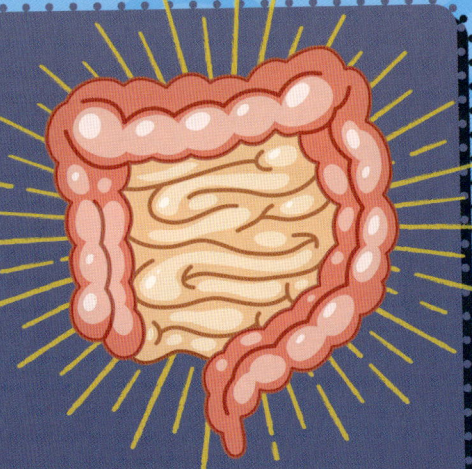

It's true that bacteria can sometimes make us sick, but there are many types of bacteria that are healthy and good for the body. Just in your gut, you can find about 100 trillion of these helpful microscopic critters! These good bacteria help you digest food, keep harmful bacteria at bay and maintain your vitally important immune system—the system that stops you from getting sick. Even though you can't see them, don't forget that you've got an army of helpful bacteria working to keep you safe and healthy!

Did you know that cockroaches can continue living for up to a week after their heads have been separated from their bodies? When a headless cockroach does eventually die, it's only because it cannot consume food or water without a mouth—it continues to breathe through tiny holes found in various places on its body!

Compared to insects, modern humans have only lived on Earth for a very short amount of time. While we've only existed here for 300,000 years, some species of insect have been living on this planet for 385 million years!

While you might squeal in both pain and delight when you're tickled by someone else, you might have noticed that it's impossible to tickle yourself. This is because your brain warns the rest of your body of what's to come, losing the element of surprise and reducing the tickling sensation.

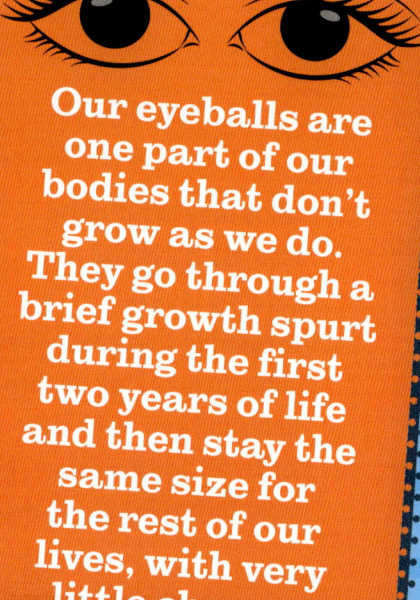

Our eyeballs are one part of our bodies that don't grow as we do. They go through a brief growth spurt during the first two years of life and then stay the same size for the rest of our lives, with very little change.

You might think that massive blue whales or giant redwood trees would be the world's largest living organisms. Well, those guesses aren't even close! In fact, the largest living organism on Earth is a fungus known as the Armillaria solidipes (or honey fungus)! Its network, which grows in the Pacific Northwest, has successfully bagged this title. It covers a massive 3.5 square miles—that's roughly the area of 1,696 football fields! It's also estimated to be 2,000 years old.

REAL-LIFE SUPER ANIMALS!

- While they're not quite headless, barreleye fish certainly look like it! Their fascinating transparent heads allow them to look up through their skull and catch sight of both prey and predators that might be lurking above them.

- The hard-to-pronounce axolotl is a small, curious salamander that is famed for its ability to regrow any limb beneath the shoulder if lost. This works not only for their limbs, but also their spinal cord, heart and even parts of their brain! They can do this as many times as needed without leaving any scarring, and the whole process can take as little as a few weeks.

- The phrase "running around like a headless chicken" was actually true for one very unlucky but fairly famous chicken back in 1945. When Colorado farmer Lloyd Olsen beheaded a chicken that became known as Mike, it miraculously continued to live for a further 18 months without its head! Mike became quite the celebrity and even went on tour.

- One of the world's toughest creatures is one you've probably never heard of. The microscopic tardigrade, otherwise known as the water bear or the moss piglet, can survive without water for up to 10 years! It also has the ability to live through extreme temperatures as low as -459°F and as high as 302°F!

- Stalk-eyed flies have a unique body feature that allows them to see around corners. Their eyes are propped up on two individual stalks, allowing them to work independently and giving the fly an incredible field of vision!

- Bats are known to have exceptional hearing and can navigate through spaces just by hearing how sound bounces off objects in their environment. They use something called "echolocation," which allows them to use sound to see! Bats make sounds so high-pitched that humans can't even hear them, and the sounds bounce off things surrounding them and help them avoid bumping into these objects as they fly.

- While we humans cannot cheat death, there's a unique species of jellyfish that has almost achieved this superpower. A seemingly immortal jellyfish called the Turritopsis dohrnii has a clever trick to prevent aging. It renews its cells completely whenever they become physically damaged or old, reverting them back to their earliest form, so that it grows into a whole new adult animal. This unbelievable power helps to make it biologically immortal!

- The blue-ringed octopus may only be as large as a golf ball, but it carries enough venom to kill 26 adult humans within minutes. Plus, there's no known cure for their venom, so their attacks are deadly!

24 Fun Facts & Amazing Activities for Curious Kids

- Professional boxers are pretty impressive, but even they have nothing on the mantis shrimp, famed for its powerful punch. These small, colorful marine creatures pack a punch that can accelerate up to 50 mph in just a fraction of a second, making it speedy enough to vaporize water and generate a miniature shock wave!

- When you first look at the thorny devil dragon lizard, you may think he has two heads. The large knob growing on its back is a fake head to confuse predators. Camouflage and spikes on its body give added protection.

- The platypus has the power to "see" electricity, and use it to locate prey! The electric fields produced by the muscle movements in its prey can be spotted by the platypus— even underwater when its eyes and ears are closed by folds of skin and its nose is closed with a watertight seal. This can help to track down even the most elusive animals!

The patterns on watermelons may look random, but did you know that all watermelons have an even number of stripes?

The Dalmatian is a beautiful, athletic dog breed known for its distinctive spotted fur. What may surprise you is that these dogs are born with plain white fur and only develop their spots after about one week.

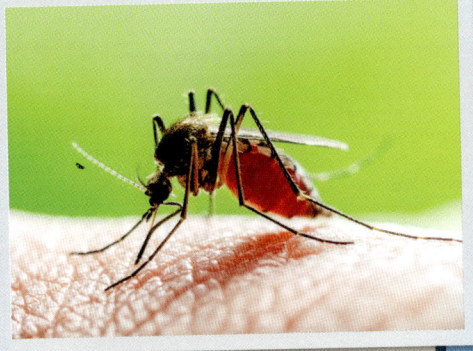

Ever had an itchy red bite left on your skin after you've been bitten by a mosquito? Those are all thanks to female mosquitoes, not male ones! While female mosquitoes bite humans and consume their blood, providing them with important nutrients to grow their eggs, male mosquitoes feed on decomposing materials and plant juices.

Did you know that the eye of an ostrich is larger than its brain? It's true! This explains why, compared to other species of bird, ostriches might not be the most intelligent—but they do have impeccable eyesight. If we're talking big-brained animals, then the sperm whale takes the cake for the largest brain volume in the animal kingdom. Their brains can weigh 17 pounds on average!

Trees that can talk? It sounds like the stuff of fairy tales, but for the acacia trees growing in African savannas, it's true! These trees have been found to communicate with one another by emitting ethylene gas. So, when an animal is chewing on their leaves, they immediately release these gases as a warning to surrounding trees that a "predator" is nearby. The other trees then know to begin producing a special toxin to steer the animal away!

On average, a chameleon's tongue is twice as long as its body! In fact, its tongue is one of the longest and fastest in the animal kingdom.

Giraffes Can't Swim   27

Cat whiskers aren't simply there for decoration—they're actually extremely sensitive and can detect a change in airflow direction, as well as vibrations in the air. This sensitivity also helps cats judge the distance between themselves and an object in their environment, helping them to navigate through a space.

While pigs say "oink!" and cows go "moo!," some animals are a bit more complicated. Guinea pigs, for example, make 11 distinct sounds. The most common of these is a high-pitched whistle or squeal, usually indicating excitement.

Despite the name, killer whales are actually not whales at all! They're part of the dolphin family, "Delphinidae," of which they are the largest member.

In the wild, giant pandas only live in China. But did you know that you can lease one? China offers pandas to zoos all over the world on a ten-year lease. However, it costs up to 1 million US dollars to house a panda for just one year, and any cubs born during this period are strictly property of China.

Giraffes cannot swim. Their long necks and legs cause them to become unbalanced in the water. Kangaroos, on the other hand, are surprisingly good swimmers. They use their legs and long tail to propel themselves along.

Taking down a large animal for dinner is quite a feat, so it's no wonder that leopards can be pretty possessive about their food. These killer cats are known to protect their prey by dragging it high up into trees, often leaving it there for days until they feel hungry enough to eat.

One downside about fossils is that they don't show us the color of a prehistoric animal's skin. While the fossil evidence we do have of dinosaurs shows that they did have different textures and colors, we'll never know what the color of their skin was. When you see dinosaurs in movies and in pictures, their skin color is merely a guess as to what they could have looked like.

While polar bears may be known for their distinctive white coats, their skin is pitch black! This black skin allows them to absorb more warmth from the sun, keeping them cozy in their Arctic homes.

There are some pretty large bones in your body, but the tiniest bones can be found in your ear. The smallest of these is just 3 millimeters long!

Garden snails may seem harmless—and they are, to humans. However, they have 14,000 teeth hiding in those tiny mouths! These chompers are used for grazing and cutting their food and sit on the snail's tongue, rather than in their gums like humans.

The glorious pink feathers on a flamingo are due to their diet of shrimp and algae, which contain a natural pink dye. When they're born, flamingos are gray or white, and only start turning pink when they're about 1 or 2 years old!

The substance that our nails and hair are made of is the same substance that makes up the horns of a rhinoceros! It's called keratin, and it's a protein that our bodies produce naturally.

Your sense of smell is a huge help when it comes to recognizing your favorite meal! The tongue is limited when it comes to its ability to pick up on different tastes—it can only taste flavors that are sweet, sour, salty, bitter and savory (some add cold and hot to this list). Your sense of smell needs to help it get creative, further enriching your tasting experience. The smell of the food is combined with your tongue's tasting ability to create layered and mouth-watering flavors. That's why your food might taste more bland when you're feeling sick or have a blocked nose—your tongue is missing its little helper!

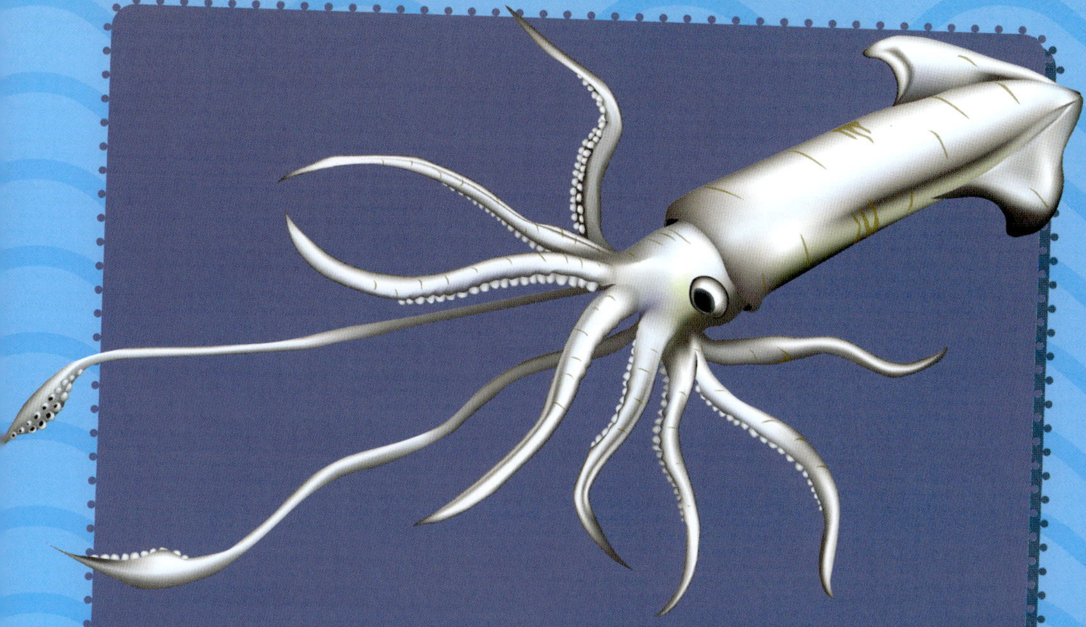

The colossal squid, the largest animal in the squid species in terms of mass, has eyes the size of basketballs! The entire length of this enormous squid's body can reach up to about 46 feet.

We suspect that dinosaurs lived pretty exciting lives, but they didn't live for very long. In fact, the oldest Tyrannosaurus rex that we know of lived to the age of about 30 before it died. That's approximately the life expectancy of a polar bear!

Ever seen a bird fly backward? Probably not, unless it was a hummingbird. These tiny creatures are the only birds that can fly backward and upside down! Unlike other birds, their wings are attached to their bodies with a ball-and-socket joint, which gives them a wider range of motion.

ACTIVITY

THE FLAVORFUL SENSORY ADVENTURE

Now that you've absorbed your first chapter of staggering facts about the wonders of biology and the body, it's time to put this new knowledge to use! Follow the instructions with a friend or family member and watch the nature of biology unfold before your very eyes.

MATERIALS

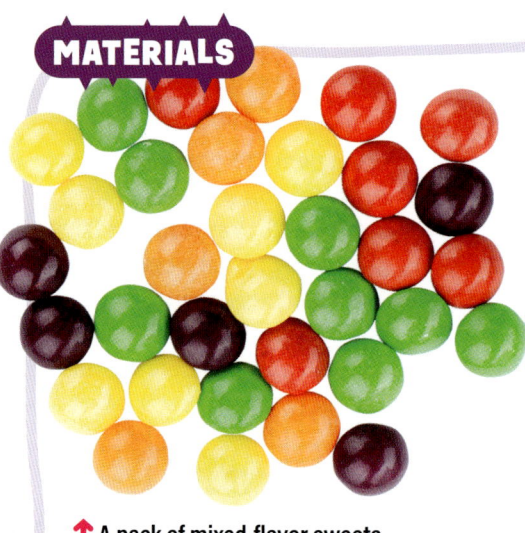

↑ A pack of mixed-flavor sweets (Skittles, Starbursts, gummy bears or anything similar)

● SAFETY TIP: Make sure that none of the people joining in have allergies to the ingredients.

● Alternatively, you can also try this experiment with other food types and flavors found in your home:

→ Flavored chips, such as barbecue, sour cream and onion, salt and vinegar or cheese

← Fruit juices (orange, apple, grape or pineapple juice)

→ Herbs and spices (powdered herbs and spices like cinnamon, cumin, paprika or ginger)

34 Fun Facts & Amazing Activities for Curious Kids

INSTRUCTIONS

1 Wash your hands.

2 Choose one participant in your group to go first. This person must close their eyes (you can also use a blindfold or a scarf to make sure they don't see what they eat) and hold their nose closed with their fingers to obstruct their sense of smell.

3 Place a piece of candy, chip, cup of juice or dash of spice in their hand. Their task is to eat it and try to identify its flavor using only their taste buds and without the use of their nose and their eyes. Write down their guess on a piece of paper.

4 Now, we reveal the smell, giving them a bit more of a clue. Allow them to stop holding their nose, but make sure they still keep their eyes closed. Ask them to guess the flavor again, and write this second guess down on the paper as well.

5 Finally, we uncover the mystery! Allow the person to open their eyes and find out the actual flavor of the food they've just tasted. Check their guesses on the paper—were they correct on the first or second guess? How far was their guess from the true flavor?

6 From here, it's the next person's turn. Continue this activity until everyone in the group has had a few tries—and remember, this is a learning journey, not a competition!

TAKE IT FURTHER

Have the group discuss their experience together.

- How did everyone's guesses change once they could smell the sweets?

- What does this teach us about how our sense of smell contributes to our tasting abilities?

- Were some flavors easier to identify than others? If so, why could that be?

There are no wrong answers, and every observation is valuable.

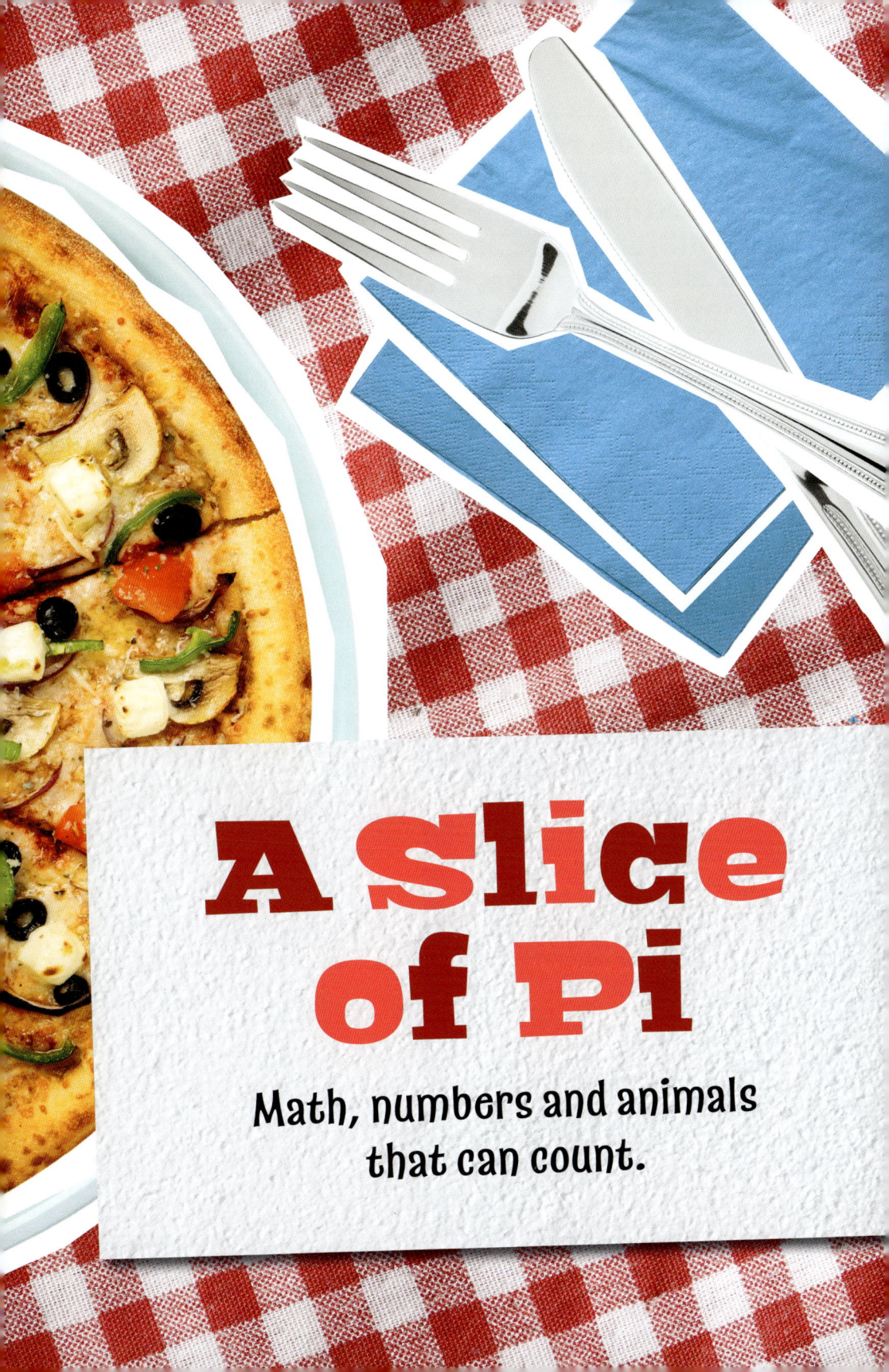

A Slice of Pi

Math, numbers and animals that can count.

A billion is such a big number, but did you know there are "illions" that come after it, too? A quadrillion, a quintillion, a sextillion, a septillion, an octillion, a nonillion, a decillion and an undecillion are all real numbers. When written out, an undecillion has a whopping 36 zeros!

1,000,000,000,000,000,000,000,000,000,000,000,000

The hour and minute hands on a clock face cross one another 11 times in 12 hours. This happens approximately every 65 minutes, not every 60 minutes, so it occurs only 22 times a day instead of 24.

Exponents are used to represent repeated multiplication of a number by itself. They provide a compact way to express large numbers and simplify calculations involving powers. For example, 2^{10} is equivalent to $2 \times 2 \times 2 \times 2 \times 2 \times 2 \times 2 \times 2 \times 2 \times 2$, which equals 1024. Exponents are also used in scientific notation to write very large or very small numbers in a more manageable form. Any number raised to the zero power is equal to 1. For example, $12345^0 = 1$.

"Googol" is a mathematics term that refers to a number that begins with 1, followed by 100 zeros. A number with a googol of zeros is called a "googolplex" and is so large that it's difficult to comprehend it!

Ever heard someone say that they'll "be there in a jiffy"? Well, it's not some made-up word—a "jiffy" is actually a real unit of time. The exact length of a jiffy varies depending on the branch of science it's used in. For example, in computer science, it's $1/60$th of a second, and in physics, it stands for the length of time it takes for light to travel 1 femtometer, or one quadrillionth of a meter! There are about three hundred thousand billion billion jiffies in a second! That's unbelievably fast!

Using mathematical probability (calculating how likely an event is to happen), we know that if there are 23 people in a room, there's a 50% chance that two of them have the same birthday.

A Slice of Pi

A TINY BUT MIGHTY NUMBER!

The smallest functional unit of space in our entire universe is known as the Planck volume, named after Max Planck, a famed German physicist. Scientists write the Planck volume as approximately 4.22×10^{-105} cubic meters. Imagine you have just over 4 apples (4.22 to be exact) and need to share them equally among all of your guests. The number of guests, however, is huge: It starts with 1 and is followed by 105 zeros! Each guest would get only a super tiny, invisible piece of an apple. That's how small Planck volume is!

The number 360 is very prominent when it comes to measurements, as 360 degrees is a full rotation. This also affects time because, when it was first recorded on the face of a circle, it became easy to divide units of time into 60 minutes and 60 seconds. But what makes the number 360 so special? The reason that historical mathematicians probably fixated on the number 360 is that it can be divided by 24 different numbers: 1, 2, 3, 4, 5, 6, 8, 9, 10, 12, 15, 18, 20, 24, 30, 36, 40, 45, 60, 72, 90, 120, 180 and 360. This means that we can split any perfect circle into a large variety of equal parts without having to use fractions.

Graham's number is one the largest numbers in math—no one can write it down or even digitally express it completely! If we tried to write each digit of Graham's number as tiny as possible so it takes only one Planck volume, our observable universe wouldn't have enough space to fit it all. Graham's number was named after mathematician Ronald Graham when it was discovered in 1971.

I'VE RUN OUT OF ROOM WRITING MY OWN NUMBER!

When written out, every odd number contains the letter "e."

one
three
five
seven
nine
eleven
thirteen
fifteen
seventeen
nineteen

40

The number **FORTY** is the only number that, when spelled out, has its letters arranged in alphabetical order.

There is evidence of human beings using mathematics about 20,000–30,000 years ago in the form of markings on animal bones. The Ishango bone, an astounding archaeological discovery, has tally marks carved into its side, which many believe is a sign that our cave-dwelling ancestors could understand basic math and make primitive measurements.

If you measure the distance around ANY circle (that's the circumference) and then measure straight across its center (that's the diameter), no matter how big or small the circle is, the ratio between these two measurements will always be the same. This special ratio is called Pi (sometimes written as π), and it's approximately 3.14. So whether it's a tiny coin or a giant pizza, the ratio of the circumference to the diameter is always Pi! Pi dates back to ancient civilizations: Egyptian, Greek and Chinese societies all had ways of determining the value of pi, with the value becoming more and more accurate with time.

Any pi fanatics can celebrate their love for the mathematical value on Pi Day, which falls on March 14th (3/14) every year. First celebrated in 1988 by physicist Larry Shaw, it has since become a popular and beloved celebration in many math-loving communities.

The following sequence of words is commonly used to help people remember the order of the first several digits of pi: "May I have a large container of coffee?" Each word in the order has the same number of letters as the first eight digits of pi (3.1415926), which is usually used as its shortened value.

Numbers are infinite and complicated, and they can sometimes blow your mind! For instance, did you know that the sum of infinite numbers can result in a finite number? If you were to continuously add half of a number to itself starting from the number 1 (1 + ½ + ¼ + . . .), you would never get an answer that amounts to more than 2!

Next time you're playing your favorite board game, take a closer look at the die. The numbers on opposite sides of a die always add up to seven!

While the concept of infinity dates all the way back to Greece in the year 500 B.C., the official symbol used to express it (∞), known as the "lemniscate," was first used by mathematician John Wallis in 1655.

The only number that is twice the value of its individual digits when added together is 18. Add 1 and 8 together, we get 9. If we double 9, we get 18. This is the only number that works in such an equation!

Percentages are reversible! It's true—take, for example, 50 and 8. If you work out 50% of 8 (half of 8 is 4), you can simultaneously find out what 8% of 50 is (also 4)! This trick works with any two numbers and can make calculating percentages much quicker and easier.

Have you ever heard of the Infinite Monkey Theorem? This idea suggests that if a monkey were allowed to randomly hit the keys of a typewriter forever, it would eventually type out all of Shakespeare's works purely by coincidence!

Ever wondered why a Rubik's Cube is so difficult to solve? It's because there are 43,252,003,274,489,856,000 possible combinations that can be made from the cube's many colorful squares, so finding just the right one is tricky and takes practice!

2

Prime numbers are special numbers that cannot be divided perfectly by any other number except for themselves and the number 1. The largest prime number we currently know of has over 24 million digits, and the smallest one is the number 2 (it's also the only even prime number!).

Sudoku is one of the most famous mathematical games. The puzzle was first introduced in Japan in 1984, but it didn't become widely popular in the Western world until 2004. It has been calculated that there are more than 6,670,903,752,021,072,936,960 ways to fill a 9 by 9 sudoku.

FIBONACCI SEQUENCE

The Fibonacci sequence is often seen in nature—the number of spirals in a pine cone, the pattern on a pineapple, the arrangement of seeds in a sunflower and the number of petals in a flower.

The Fibonacci sequence is a series of numbers in which each number is the sum of the two preceding ones. It starts with 0 and 1, and each subsequent number is found by adding the two numbers that came before it. The sequence begins as follows: 0, 1, 1, 2, 3, 5, 8, 13, 21, 34, 55, 89 . . .

Concentric circles are a set of circles that all share the same center point but are different sizes, placing them perfectly inside one another. We can see this pattern in the rings of tree trunks, in ripples on the water in a pond and in the layers of an onion.

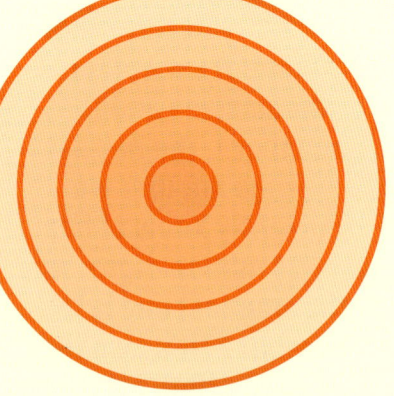

Ever wonder why beehives are constructed from hexagons? The answer is a little complex and starts with needing a shape that can be replicated easily and joined together without any gaps. The square, the triangle and the hexagon could all suit this purpose, but because bees are highly focused on doing things efficiently, the hexagon best suits all their needs. It has the smallest perimeter per area, which means it uses less wax and energy from the bees. Bees can also calculate angles and make measurements, which helps in their building processes!

The cicada is another insect that uses mathematics. They are known to stay underground for long periods of time before they come out to mate, creating tunnels in their wingless forms and feeding on sap found in the roots of trees. Sometimes they come out after 13 years and sometimes they wait 17 years. Biologists have noticed that both of these intervals of time are prime numbers, and they believe that the cicadas have adapted to these particular life cycles to avoid predators that are more likely to have even-numbered life cycles.

1,2,3,4,3,2,1

A palindrome number is a number that has the same sequence of digits whether you read it backward or forward. An example would be the number 21,312. We see such numbers all the time, but now you know what to call them!

In Thailand, the number 555 is often texted to indicate that something is funny (it's the same as saying "LOL" in the Western world). This is because, in Thai 5 is pronounced as "ha," meaning that 555 can be said aloud as "hahaha."

You may know that chess is a complicated game that involves prediction, math and concentration. But did you know that there are more possible iterations of a chess game than there are existing atoms in the observable universe? In fact, if you multiply the number of atoms in the observable universe (10^{81}) by the total number of hairs on all the human heads in the world (10^{15}) and then by the number of seconds that passed since dinosaurs became extinct (2×10^{15}), the result will still be smaller than the number of all possible chess games (10^{120}). That is quite impressive for just 32 pieces on a board.

The idea that 13 is an unlucky number has roots in the Christian religion. On the night Jesus was crucified, 13 guests were present at the Last Supper, and many consider Judas Iscariot, Jesus's betrayer, to be the 13th guest. The impact of this unluckiest of numbers was significant. Even today, some buildings don't have a 13th floor, some restaurants don't have a 13th table and some people will even go so far as to avoid getting married or buying a house on the 13th day of the month!

Favorite and least favorite numbers tend to differ between cultures. For example, the number 4 is considered to be highly unlucky and symbolic of death in Chinese and Japanese culture.

Seven is one of the most popular numbers. In a poll conducted in 2017, math writer Alex Bellos found that, of 44,000 people surveyed, nearly 10% of them selected 7 as their favorite.

A number can only be wholly divided by 3 without leaving a remainder if all of its digits added together equals a value that can be divided by 3. For example, 27 can be divided by 3, because 2 + 7 = 9, which is also divisible by 3!

The earliest known calculating tool that is still used today, other than our fingers, is the abacus. This device was invented in China, and its use dates back to 300 B.C. Although it looks simple, it can be used to calculate additions, subtractions, multiplications, divisions and even calculations using decimal places. Some parts of the world still use the abacus today!

Roman numerals (I, II, III, IV, V, etc.) are a collection of symbols that the ancient Romans used to express the number sequence. Unlike our modern numbers, however, these numerals have no expression for the value of zero!

The ratio 3:2:1 is an easy way to remember the perfect cookie recipe! In this ratio, 3 parts will be flour, 2 parts will be fat (oil or butter) and 1 part will be sugar. Who knew mathematics could be so tasty?

Did you know there's a way to color every single flat map in the world using only four colors, without any two adjacent regions sharing the same color? This is called the Four Color Map Theorem, and it was finally proven in 1976. Proving the theory was quite a unique process during that time as it relied heavily on calculations made by computers (which initiated topical debate about how computers could and should help prove mathematical theorems).

The pattern on a soccer ball (called a football in some countries) is made up of pentagons and hexagons. You'll usually spot 12 pentagons and 20 hexagons.

ACTIVITY

THE FANTASTIC FOUR COLOR CHALLENGE

Now that you have gained boundless knowledge about the fascinating world of mathematics, we can put you and your family and friends to the test with this fun, challenging and creative task! After all, you don't need years of study or a fancy degree to enjoy math.

The activity described below exemplifies the Four Color Map Theorem we learned about on pg. 51. Today, we'll try it out for ourselves and see if it's true!

MATERIALS

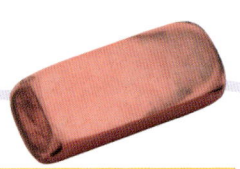

↑ A pencil and an eraser

← Four different colored markers or crayons

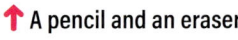

A few sheets of white paper (or cardboard)

INSTRUCTIONS

1 We begin with a creative drawing session. Start by drawing a large map on your sheet of paper with a pencil—this can be a map of your neighborhood, your town or an imaginary world.

2 Now for the fun part! It's time to color in your map, but there's a catch—you only have four colors, and no two areas (countries or regions on your map) that share a side can be the same color. The borders of two areas sharing a color can touch at a point, but if they share an entire side, they need to be different colors. Can you manage it?

3 When everyone has completed their maps, have a look around and see if anyone has found a map that they think breaks the Four Color Map Theorem. Check them all together.

TAKE IT FURTHER

For an extra challenge, try to create a map that you think would need more than four colors to fill in. If you think you've designed one, let someone else have a go at coloring your map and see if they can color it in with only the four colors.

It's Elemental

Chemistry, atoms and 2,000 helium balloons.

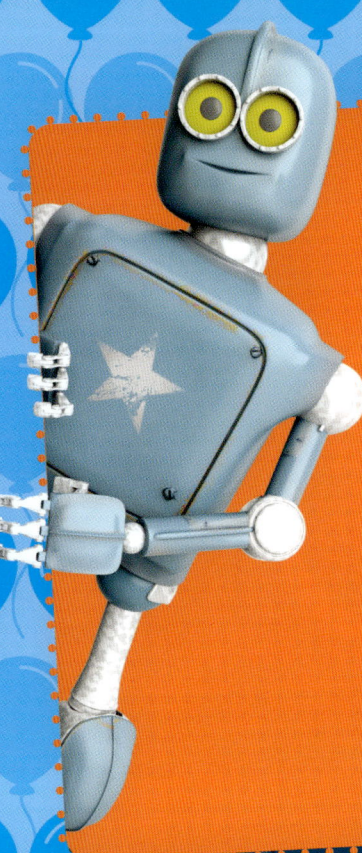

You've heard of Iron Man, but if there was a superhero named "Steel Man," he'd be much stronger! Steel is around 1,000 times stronger than iron's purest form.

It is estimated that 90% of the visible universe is made of hydrogen! It is also the only element with no neutrons, making it the simplest element in the universe.

Speaking of the universe: all hydrogen atoms were created during the birth of the universe. This means that every hydrogen atom in your body is likely billions of years old!

Lead used to be commonly used in face whitening makeup and paint for children's toys. Thankfully, these practices were stopped in most countries when the highly toxic properties of lead were discovered!

Coming into contact with radioactivity is incredibly dangerous, but did you know the bananas you eat as a snack are considered slightly radioactive? Unbelievable as it might seem, this is because they contain a very small amount of an isotope called potassium-40.

It's incredibly difficult to put out a magnesium fire. If you try to put it out using water, this will produce hydrogen, only intensifying the flames. A normal carbon dioxide fire extinguisher can't be used, because magnesium can still burn in pure nitrogen and pure carbon dioxide! In fact, the only way to put out this kind of fire is to use a chemical fire extinguisher or cover the fire with sand.

Nickel was once commonly used to make coins, but we made a switch to using cheaper metals when it was discovered that many people find nickel irritating on their skin.

80
Hg
Mercury
200 592

Mercury is the only metal that remains a liquid at room temperature.

Did you know that you can die from drinking too much water? Staying well hydrated is essential for all life, but drinking too much water (about 4 liters within the space of an hour) causes the sodium levels in your body to drop rapidly and allows water to enter the brain. This can cause brain swelling and lead to seizures, trouble breathing and, ultimately, death.

The boiling point of water changes at different altitudes. At sea level, water boils at 212°F. But if you were to heat a pot of water on top of Mount Everest, for example, it would boil at just 158°F!

Corrosion is a destructive process where metals react with their environment. Titanium is not only highly resistant to any form of corrosion, including from seawater and chlorine, but it is the strongest of all metals in relation to its weight. It is, in fact, as strong as steel, even though it is 45% lighter!

Dry ice never becomes a liquid. This pretty cool substance is actually solidified carbon dioxide—yes, the stuff you exhale! When you heat it up, instead of becoming a liquid, dry ice immediately becomes a gas (a process called sublimation).

All flames are dangerous to touch, but did you know the color of a flame can actually tell you how hot it is? If a flame is red, it's between 1,112 and 1,472°F. Orange flames are a bit hotter, between 1,472 and 2,192°F. Blue flames are the hottest of all—they can reach 3,002°F!

That beautiful, expensive glass vase your parent won't let you touch may look like a solid, but it's actually not! That's right—in its purest form, glass is an amorphous substance, meaning that it's somewhere between a solid and a liquid.

Besides hydrogen and helium, all the elements in our universe were created inside stars through a process known as nuclear fusion.

Ever wondered why some doorknobs and handrails in public buildings are made of copper or brass? This is actually a hygiene precaution—you see, copper is a natural antibacterial! This element has also been used to line parts of ships for centuries so that barnacles and mussels do not stick to the bottom.

Baking is a form of chemistry. Baking bread involves many chemical reactions. One of them is when yeast turns sugars into carbon dioxide, which makes the bread expand. A reaction known as the Maillard reaction also occurs, which makes the bread turn golden brown and tasty!

Modern chemistry has its roots in ancient alchemy, which combined practical knowledge with a philosophical approach to nature and all matter. Alchemists mostly aimed to turn common metals, like lead and copper, into gold, but this goal was never achieved. However, important discoveries about the elements and their capabilities were made in the process.

It's Elemental 61

Did you know your body naturally contains a large amount of carbon? Carbon in its purest form occurs as graphite. Our bodies contain enough carbon to provide graphite for the creation of 9,000 pencils!

If you mix together ½ liter of alcohol and ½ liter of water, the resulting liquid will be less than 1 liter in volume. But how is this possible? Well, when you mix water and alcohol, they form hydrogen bonds with each other, and the alcohol molecules slip into spaces between water molecules. You can visualize if you add water to a full box of pebbles. While the box of pebbles was full in the first place, you manage to add more to it.

Ever wondered how tiny an atom is? To give you an idea, one bucket of water contains more atoms than there are buckets of water in the Atlantic Ocean!

The planet Mars appears red because its surface comprises large amounts of iron oxide, known more commonly as rust. The atmosphere on the planet contains both water and carbon dioxide, which provide oxygen for the iron to react with, resulting in its vibrant red color.

The molecule capsaicin is what makes hot peppers spicy and irritating to the tongue. Mammals react to this molecule, but birds don't have the receptor needed to experience it, meaning they can consume hot peppers without feeling a thing!

While both are equally painful, bee stings and wasp stings are quite different due to the pH of the venom in each sting. Bee venom is acidic, which is why rubbing an alkaline substance such as baking soda on it may help relieve the effects. The pH of wasp venom is alkaline, but only by a narrow margin.

BREATHE IN!

- About 28% of the world's oxygen is produced by rainforests. Tiny organisms called plankton that float in our oceans are, however, the largest contributor: they produce at least half of all the oxygen on Earth.

- While oxygen is necessary for a fire to occur, as it supports combustion, it cannot burn on its own and is not inherently a flammable element.

- Oxygen is a gas at room temperature under usual conditions, but it can actually melt and boil, too! This element melts at -361.82°F and boils at -297.31°F.

- We need oxygen to survive, but it is possible to have too much of it! Breathing in too much oxygen causes a condition known as the bends, and it's actually something astronauts and scuba divers need to be very wary of. When these individuals inhale too much oxygen too quickly, tiny bubbles can form in their blood, which can be fatal.

- While oxygen might appear not to have any color as a gas, it actually turns a pale blue when it becomes liquid or solid. This is because the pressure forces the molecules closer together, making their true color more visible to the naked eye.

It's Elemental

BREATHE IN!
(CONTINUED)

- Oxygen is the most common element on Earth, making up large quantities of our oceans, atmosphere and Earth's crust.

- There are several forms of oxygen. The type we inhale is actually two oxygen atoms bonded together (O_2). On the other hand, O_3 is three oxygen atoms bonded together, ozone. This is not safe to breathe.

- Did you know that oxygen dissolves in water? There is actually oxygen in both fresh water and seawater! Fresh water contains roughly 6.04 ml of oxygen per liter, while seawater contains 4.95 ml of oxygen per liter.

PERIODIC TABLE

The periodic table was invented by **Dmitri Mendeleev** in 1869 in an attempt to arrange all the elements systematically. While other scientists had tried to make tables such as this in the past, Mendeleev's is the most widely approved among the scientific community.

The periodic table is constantly under review and subject to updates and improvements. When Dmitri Mendeleev first presented it, it only included 63 elements. Today, there are 118 elements—and counting!

I LOVE ORGANIZING THINGS. PERIODICALLY.

In 2016, the newest elements were added to the periodic table. Research groups from Japan, the US and Russia discovered elements numbered 113, 115, 117 and 118, and three of them were named after the places in which they were discovered: nihonium, moscovium and tennessine. The fourth, oganesson, was named after a nuclear physicist.

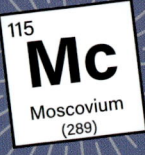
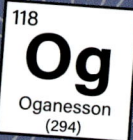

The elements in the periodic table can be found throughout the universe. The elements found on Mars or in another galaxy are the same elements that make up the matter on Earth.

The only letter in the alphabet that does not appear on the periodic table is J.

Around 95 of the 118 elements on the periodic table are metals. Some elements are more difficult to classify, however, because the distinctions between metals, nonmetals and metalloids is not globally agreed upon.

The magnificent fireworks show that lights up the sky on New Year's Eve is nothing but a display of chemical reactions. Copper gives off a blue color, sodium gives off yellow, barium gives off green and strontium gives off red.

Did you know our kitchens are like science labs, full of color-changing magic? The juices of many foods we eat, like blueberries, red cabbage, red onion or spices like turmeric, can change color when mixed with things like lemon juice (which is acidic) or baking soda (which is alkaline). These foods can transform from their usual colors into a whole different spectrum, turning cooking into an exciting science demonstration (see pg. 72)!

Gold is a pretty malleable element— just .03 ounces can be hammered down into a thin sheet roughly 10.8 square feet in size! It can also be made so thin that it looks transparent.

Most of the elements on the periodic table occur naturally, but there are a few that are man-made. The first ever man-made element, technetium, was discovered in 1937 in Italy and was found to be present in spent nuclear fuel rods.

43
Tc
Technetium
(98)

The gold medals awarded at the Olympic Games only contain about .02 ounces of gold and are mostly made of silver.

A famous chemist, Glenn Seaborg, had every aspect of his work address represented on the periodic table—his name, his lab and the city, state and country in which it was located: **Sg** (seaborgium—the element named after Seaborg himself), **Lr** (lawrencium—the element named after the Lawrence Berkeley National Laboratory), **Bk** (berkelium—an element named after Berkeley, the city), **Cf** (californium—named after California), **Am** (americium—named after the U.S.).

106	103	97	98	95
Sg	**Lr**	**Bk**	**Cf**	**Am**
Seaborgium	Lawrencium	Berkelium	Californium	Americium
(269)	(266)	(247)	(251)	(243)

It's Elemental

ACTIVITY

FIND YOUR (PH) BALANCE

With your newfound knowledge about chemistry and the elements found in the periodic table, you are ready to explore chemistry hands-on! Carry out this experiment at home with family or friends using items and ingredients found in your kitchen and watch the magic of pH unfold before your very eyes.

The pH scale is used to identify how acidic or alkaline a liquid is; pH indicators change color depending on the pH of the solution they are in.

There are several items you can use to create your own pH indicators at home, all of which can typically be found in the kitchen.

MATERIALS

↑ Hot water

↓ A jug that can withstand hot water

↑ A colander

↓ Six clear cups or glasses

72 Fun Facts & Amazing Activities for Curious Kids

FIND YOUR (PH)BALANCE (CONTINUED)

INSTRUCTIONS

1 Allow your indicator liquid to cool for a while if necessary. When it is cool enough to handle, use a colander to separate the liquid from solid if using cabbage, onion or berries. The more saturated the color is, the better you will see the color change. Just try not to make it too dark.

2 Next, place your clear cups in a row, about an inch apart from each other, and pour equal amounts of the liquid you made into each cup.

3 Now, it's time to prepare your testers. You can have some lemon juice, distilled vinegar, some tap or carbonated water, a small amount of dish soap or hand soap and a small amount of baking soda.

4 Let's make the magic happen! Carefully pour a small amount of each tester into a clear cup containing your pH indicator. Observe as a color change occurs in each cup, and write down how the liquid reacts to each tester. Which testers bring about the greatest color change? Which testers cause little to no change in color?

TAKE IT FURTHER

Arrange all the cups in order from most acidic on the left to most alkaline on the right based on their color. For example, here is a general guide for interpreting the color changes if you use red cabbage as an indicator:

- red (highly acidic)
- pink (moderately acidic)
- no color change (neutral)
- blue (slightly alkaline)
- green (moderately alkaline)
- yellow (highly alkaline)

Other pH indicators from our list might show different colors—try them to find out.

Out of This World

Space, physics and golf on the moon.

Believe it or not, it's possible to freeze and boil water at the same time! It sounds unfathomable, but if you reduce the air pressure and temperature, this unthinkable feat of physics can be achieved! This is called "triple point," and for water, it occurs at a temperature of 32.018°F and a pressure of 0.006 atm (atmosphere).

I ONCE STUCK MY TONGUE OUT FOR A PHOTO!

Ever wished you could time-travel? Well, flying aboard an airplane is probably as close as you can get today! With Einstein's theory of relativity, he stated that moving objects experience the effects of time more slowly than stationary objects. An experiment performed in 1971, known as the Hafele-Keating experiment, proved this by showing that atomic clocks aboard airplanes lagged slightly when compared to atomic clocks in one fixed location.

In the year 46 BC, **Julius Caesar** decided to change the calendar to the 365-day year version we use today (which represents Earth making one orbit around the sun). In order to get the calendar in sync, he ordered there to be a 445-day-long year to catch up with the seasons—the longest calendar year in recorded history!

People in different cultures tend to have varying ideas about how time works. For example, in the Western world, we picture time as linear, and if we were to draw a timeline, we would draw it from left to right. However, people who speak languages that are written in the opposite direction (like Arabic) picture time as moving from right to left. The Aymara, a tribe of people living in the Andes Mountains think of the future as being behind them, with the past laid out in front of them. Some cultures use directions like north, south, east and west to describe time too!

Mercury is the fastest planet in our solar system, making its way around the sun in only 88 days. It shoots across its orbit at almost 29.2 miles per second, compared to Earth's 18.64 miles per second or 66,487 miles per hour, as you learned at the start of our quest (pg. 8)!

Out of This World   79

One day on Venus is longer than one year on Venus! This is due to the fact that this planet turns incredibly slowly on its axis, and takes a total of 243 Earth days to make a full turn. This means that a day on Venus is equal to 243 days on Earth. However, it takes only 225 Earth days to orbit the sun, so a year on Venus is 18 Earth days shorter than one day on Venus!

Trees on Earth outnumber stars in our galaxy! That's right; there are approximately 3 trillion trees on planet Earth and only an estimated 300 billion stars in the Milky Way!

Musical instruments can't make any sound in outer space. That's because space has no atmosphere, which means the sound has no way of being transmitted. Even when pieces of space debris crash into each other or stars explode, it makes absolutely no noise!

We know that the Sun is unbelievably hot, but the Earth's core is as hot as the Sun's surface! Way down there, temperatures can soar all the way to 9,932°F.

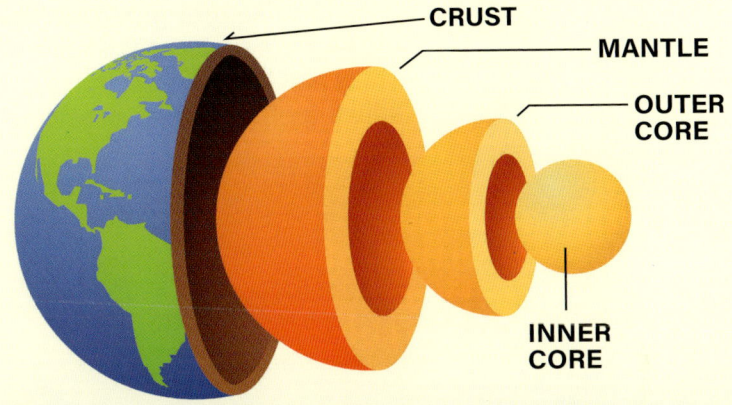

While it may look like they do, several planets don't have a solid surface that humans could walk on. Jupiter, Saturn, Neptune and Uranus—known as the Jovian planets—are made up mostly of helium and hydrogen and therefore don't have solid surfaces like Earth and Mars. They're basically giant balls of gas!

Did you know that golf is the only sport that has been played on the moon? The commander of the Apollo 14 mission, **Alan Shepard,** famously hit a couple of golf balls using a Wilson six-iron head attached to a lunar sample scoop handle in 1971! However, aboard the International Space Station, astronauts had the opportunity to take part in other sports too, like zero-gravity football and basketball. As you can guess, they had to modify the rules to adjust for the absence of gravity.

The mass of the Sun takes up 99.86% of our solar system! You could say it's the "star" of the show, a pretty "big" deal!

All the planets in our solar system, and nearly all the asteroids, orbit around the sun in the same direction. This direction would be considered counterclockwise if you were to stand way above the Earth's North Pole and look out into space.

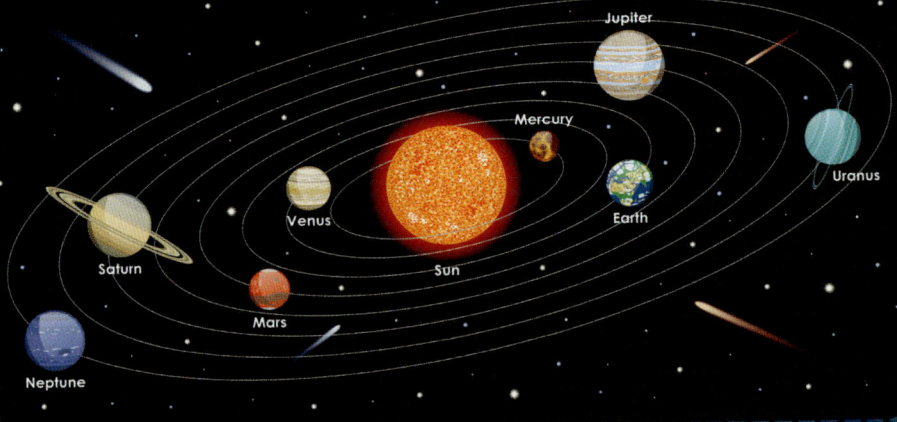

Want to see how wavelengths work? Hold one end of a rope while your friend holds the other. Slowly move one end up and down and you'll see a demonstration of how long wavelengths work. For short wavelengths, rapidly wiggle your end of the rope up and down.

Think Mount Everest is high? An asteroid in space called Vesta has a mountain reaching 13.67 miles in height, making it the tallest mountain known to humankind!

Did you know that it rains on other planets? It's often quite different from the rain we experience on Earth. For example, Venus experiences drops of sulfuric acid falling to its surface instead of water droplets, and the heat on Venus is so intense the droplets evaporate before they even land!

Clouds may look light and fluffy, but all that water retention actually makes them incredibly heavy. The average cloud can weigh over 1 million pounds!

Every comet is as old as our solar system. These masses of sand, ice and carbon dioxide are simply leftovers from when our solar system came into being 4.5 billion years ago. Most of them, if frozen, would be the size of a whole town!

Did you know that thunder is the effect of a shock wave? Whenever a lightning bolt strikes, air rapidly expands and contracts, creating a shock wave that ripples through the sky and creates that thunderous boom!

Lightning bolts exude an immense amount of energy. In fact, one single bolt of lightning can contain the amount of energy required to power a 25-watt light bulb for over three months!

84 Fun Facts & Amazing Activities for Curious Kids

Nothing in the universe can travel faster than the speed of light. It moves at about 621,370,000 miles per hour, while the speed of sound is only 767.4 miles per hour! That's why you see lightning much sooner than you hear thunder, even though the sight and sound come from the same source.

Halley's Comet is one of the most well-known comets, named after the astronomer and mathematician Edmond Halley. It comes into our solar system only once every 75 years, and it was last visible from Earth in 1986. That means we won't see it again until 2061—how old will you be when that happens?

ANY COMMENTS ABOUT MY COMET?

While Celsius and Fahrenheit are two very different measures of temperature, they converge at the value of -40. Yes, -40 degrees Celsius is the same as -40 degrees Fahrenheit!

It may sound impossible, but, in theory, a Formula 1 race car could drive upside down in a tunnel at 124.3 miles per hour! The downforce produced by this particular vehicle's aerodynamic design would help it stick to the ceiling and keep driving forward.

Not all planets in our solar system rotate in the same way Earth does. Venus rotates in the opposite direction as Earth. While we turn counterclockwise, Venus turns clockwise! Uranus is the only planet in our solar system that rotates on its side.

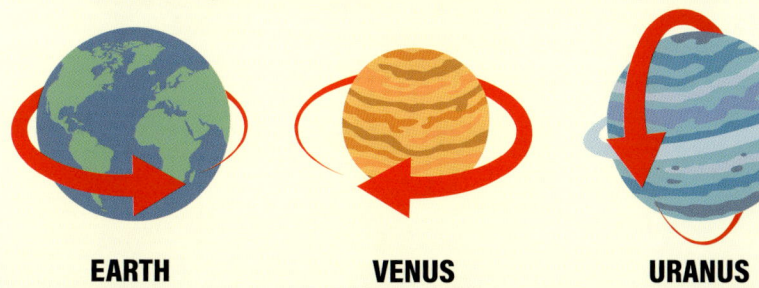

EARTH **VENUS** **URANUS**

Galaxies are constantly moving! The closest galaxy to ours, the **Andromeda Galaxy**, is expected to collide with our own (the Milky Way) in 3.75 billion years. They will then form a giant elliptical (smooth, oval-shaped) galaxy.

MERCURY

VENUS

MARS

JUPITER

SATURN

NEPTUNE

All planets in our solar system, except Earth and Uranus, are named after Roman gods and goddesses. Uranus is named after the Greek god of the sky. Earth, however, is an Old English/Germanic word that means "ground."

Sun · Mercury · Venus · Earth · Mars · Jupiter · Saturn · Uranus · Neptune

Until 2006, our solar system consisted of nine planets. However, this dropped to eight when the International Astronomical Union made its definitions of a planet more strict, deciding to effectively demote Pluto to a dwarf planet.

The largest water discovery ever made was a massive cloud of water vapor located 10 billion light-years away from Earth, which appears to hold 140 trillion times more water than all our oceans put together!

There are 1,800 thunderstorms happening at the same time on Earth at any given moment. This amounts to 16 million storms every year.

We've heard of black holes, but did you know there are white holes, too? White holes are theoretical objects that spew out matter instead of sucking it in the way black holes do. While we like to theorize about their existence, we've never actually seen one and don't expect to find one in our universe.

Over a billion years ago, a day on Earth was only about 18 hours long. This was because, back then, the moon was farther away than it is today. Now, days are longer because gravity from the moon has caused the rotation of the Earth to slow down, adding more hours of daylight to our lives. Continue reading to learn how many days dinosaurs were waiting to celebrate the New Year (pg. 134)!

Because stars and space matter are so far away from us here on Earth, looking up at the night sky is like looking back into the past. The light we see from stars takes a very long time to reach us, so when we look at them, we see what they looked like years—even centuries—ago.

In a surprising feat of physics, a crumpled piece of paper is actually stronger than a flat piece of paper. The creases in the paper absorb force and evenly distribute it across the surface, adding to its strength!

Is teleportation possible? In recent years, scientists have found a way to teleport very small singular particles on a subatomic level using something called quantum entanglement. This technology, however, is very far away from reaching a point where it could teleport humans!

While we all aim to make our mark in life, anyone who has been on the moon has left one in a very literal sense. Because there is no wind on the moon, there has been no disturbance to the footprints and rover tire tracks left there since our last visit. In fact, it's believed that those marks will remain on the moon for millions of years to come.

While the moon has large craters to show evidence of its many collisions with asteroids, meteors and space debris, the Earth has also had its fair share of collisions. However, on Earth, we have tsunamis, soil erosion, volcanic eruptions, earthquakes and other natural disasters that slowly erode all evidence of our impacts with space matter. Because the moon has no atmosphere, none of these events can occur, leaving it spotted with large craters!

Saturn is the only planet in our solar system that is less dense than water. That means if you put it in a (very, very large) bathtub, it would float!

The largest moon in our solar system belongs to Jupiter, and its name is Ganymede. It's bigger than Mercury and Pluto!

Theoretically, astronauts could propel themselves through space by exhaling! Breathing out would propel them in the opposite direction, similarly to how air escaping from a balloon would propel a balloon car!

ACTIVITY

START YOUR ENGINES

Now that you have gained boundless knowledge about space and physics, actual events happening around you might start to make a lot more sense. For example, a car's engine is quite complicated, and whether it works or not depends on many factors that are meticulously and perfectly calculated. But did you know there are a lot of simple, physics-based ways you can make toy cars move on their own? That's right! This easy activity that you can perform at home will show you how.

MATERIALS

← A paper straw

← Some tape or a rubber band

← Lots of lung capacity!

↑ A toy car (you can build one using LEGO bricks or cardboard, like this)

← A balloon

INSTRUCTIONS

1 Insert the paper straw into the open hole of the balloon and secure it with tape. Then, place the straw upright facing backward on the back of the car, with the balloon on the top end, and use several pieces of tape to secure it.

2 Blow into the straw until the balloon is inflated and pinch the balloon so the air stays inside.

3 Now put the car on the floor or table, release the balloon and watch your little car zoot around, powered by the air!

4 Think about what changes you can make so your car goes farther. Adding a bigger balloon or two? Making the car heavier or lighter?

TAKE IT FURTHER

You can explore other ways to move your car! Attach one magnet to your car, and hold the other magnet in your hand. Move the magnets closer and, depending on the polarization of the magnets, they will repel or attract and move the car at the same time.

Try finding other ways you can propel your toy car forward. Whether you will be using rubber bands or attaching sails to your car, the goal is to enjoy exploring the fun world of physics!

Totally Tectonic

Geoscience, culture and the rock we call home.

Although roughly 71% of Earth's surface is covered with water, all the water on Earth by volume makes up just 0.02% of the planet.

The amount of water that exists on Earth has never changed. Today, we have the same amount of water that was present on our planet millions of years ago, when dinosaurs were around.

NWA 11119 is the oldest meteorite formed from cooled magma or lava that has been found on Earth. It is estimated to be roughly 4.6 billion years old. That's older than Earth itself and almost as old as our solar system! The "NWA" in its name refers to where it was found—Northwest Africa—and "11119" is its identification number.

Ever tried to guess what's hidden beneath the wrapping paper of your Christmas present before opening it? Well, this is kind of how we've guessed what's below the surface of the earth! When we talk about the earth's crust, mantle and core, we're discussing what's considered a working theory. Known as the "layered Earth theory," this calculated estimation states that the crust is the part of the earth that we exist upon, the outermost layer, while the mantle is a much hotter layer that lies underneath and the core is located at the very center of the planet. However, because we've never been able to dig that deep into the earth's surface, this is only a theory. The reality could be completely different!

Did you know that you'll always be seven years ahead of Ethiopia? While the rest of the world uses the Gregorian calendar, this African country calculates the start of their year differently, which also leads them to celebrate New Year's on September 11th and Christmas on January 7th. For them, the year 2000 started in our 2007!

Ethiopia

Totally Tectonic 97

Long (long long long) ago, Earth's continents were connected as part of a supercontinent called Pangaea. The earth's crust is split into several large tectonic plates and, about 335 million years ago, these plates were joined together to form Pangaea. However, because these tectonic plates are always moving, the massive land mass ultimately split apart about 175 million years ago to form the continents we know today. Scientists predict that one day, the movement of the tectonic plates may once again form another giant continent, which will be called Pangaea Proxima.

The Atacama Desert in Chile is one of the driest places on Earth, where no rain has fallen for hundreds of years. Surprisingly, certain species of bacteria and fungi have still been able to survive there.

Iceland is growing by nearly 5 centimeters every year. This is because it sits right where the North American and Eurasian tectonic plates meet, and as these plates move apart, the land splits and magma rises to the surface, resulting in volcanic activity and the formation of new crust.

A valley named Oymyakon in the Russian republic of Yakutia is the coldest inhabited place on Earth. Also known as the Pole of Cold, this valley has temperatures that drop as low as -94°F! While these conditions may seem unlivable, a small community of about 500 Siberian people herd, hunt and fish in this region.

Ōkunoshima is an island in Japan where the only permanent residents are rabbits!

Ever heard of an island within a lake, on an island within a lake, on an island? This rare phenomenon is called a "third-order island." There is one in the Philippines called Vulcan Point. To break it down, the small rocky island of Vulcan Point is located in Taal Volcano Main Crater Lake, which is situated on the larger Taal Island, which is an island in Taal Lake. Taal Lake itself is located on the island of Luzon.

Did you know it can rain underground? Located in Vietnam, Hang Son Doong is the world's largest natural cave. It features a subterranean river so vast that it has its own localized weather system. Rain clouds can form inside the cave's hollows.

Adopted in 1981, Belize's national flag has more colors than any other national flag in the world. The 12 colors depict the country's coat of arms on a blue background, with red stripes along the top and bottom of the flag. It was adopted after the nation gained its independence from the United Kingdom.

We all have dream destinations, but it seems that many people—approximately 90 million every year—all dream of traveling to France. Indeed, it's the most-visited country in the world, tailed closely by Spain and the United States.

South America, the location of the Amazon Rainforest, is often incorrectly thought of as the most forested area in the world. Actually, that honor goes to Russia, with its boreal forest region boasting about 2 billion acres of trees!

One of the most powerful volcanic eruptions in recorded history caused a "year without summer" due to its release of enormous amounts of sulfur dioxide and ash into the Earth's atmosphere. This eruption of the Indonesian volcano Tambora took place in 1815, and its effects impacted global weather patterns. The temperature dropped around the world and many harvests failed, resulting in a global food shortage. Volcanoes can erupt in several different ways: effusive eruptions happen when lava flows like a river, while explosive eruptions blast out ash and rocks over 12.4 miles through the air. You can witness your very own at-home volcanic eruption using lemons, soap and baking soda on pg. 110!

Zealandia, a large sunken continent, was submerged after breaking away from Australia approximately 60-85 million years ago. New Zealand and New Caledonia are the only parts of Zealandia that stay above water, but a staggering 94% of it is underwater.

Totally Tectonic 103

Did you know that Bangkok, the capital of Thailand, has another name? In fact, it's the longest name of any city in the world, formerly known as Krung Thep Mahanakhon Amon Rattanakosin Mahinthara Ayuthaya Mahadilok Phop Noppharat Ratchathani Burirom Udomratchaniwet Mahasathan Amon Piman Awatan Sathit Sakkathattiya Witsanukam Prasit! Eventually, the city chose to change its name to the shorter and more convenient "Bangkok" in place of its 21-word name.

WHOA, SNOW WAY!

Because the Sahara Desert gets little rain, you'd never imagine that this part of the world would be capable of experiencing snowfall. However, this seeming impossibility became real in 2018, and, for just one day, the hot sand was covered in glistening white snow! It quickly melted under the baking-hot sun.

Today, we know the Sahara Desert as the world's largest hot desert, spanning over 3.6 million square miles. But did you know that it used to be a tropical rainforest? Just 6,000 years ago, this barren land was a lush rainforest with thick vegetation, a tropical climate and lots of rain!

Sand dunes in the Sahara Desert can reach a height of 590 feet—roughly twice the height of Big Ben's tower in London!

Think the walk from your bedroom to the kitchen is long? Maybe don't visit the Great Wall of China anytime soon. At a mind-boggling 13,171 miles long, it would take you about 6 months to walk along its entire length, and that's assuming you walk nonstop without any breaks. Originally built during the third century BC as a means to protect China's territory from invaders, it took over 2,000 years to fully construct it!

Places closer to the equator are subject to slightly weaker gravity. It's easy to assume that the pull of gravity would be equally strong everywhere on Earth, but the centrifugal force from the rotation of the earth is at its strongest near the equator, interfering with the strength of gravity.

Point Nemo is a place in the ocean that is the farthest away from any land. If you were to go here, you'd be closer to the astronauts in space than to any people living on Earth! The International Space Station orbits Earth from approximately 254 miles away, while the closest land dwellers to Point Nemo are over 1,616 miles away!

Plastiglomerate is a newly discovered kind of rock that is formed from plastic waste, sediment, shells and debris. The first samples of this rock were found in Hawaii in 2006, and the discovery is a clear indication of how plastic pollution affects our natural environment.

Vatican City is the world's smallest country by land area. This tiny country is located entirely within the city of Rome, Italy.

LINGUISTIC LABYRINTHS

- The world is a vast, diverse and fascinating place, and it is our human differences that make life on Earth so interesting. There are more than 7,000 languages spoken across the globe. Mandarin Chinese, Spanish, English and Hindi are the languages with the highest number of speakers, but some languages only have one or two living speakers! While it may have many speakers, Mandarin Chinese is widely considered the most difficult language to learn.

- Of all the languages in the world, the Bible has been translated into 3,384 of them, making it the most widely translated book available. However, Agatha Christie takes the title of the world's most widely translated author.

- The Turkish village of Kuşköy still uses an incredibly rare whistling language known as "bird language" in a centuries-old tradition that has now been listed on the UNESCO list of Intangible Cultural Heritage. While the language isn't used to communicate with birds, the sounds have been said to mimic bird calls. The high-pitched noises help speakers communicate over the region's steep mountain ranges and across long distances.

- As far as alphabets go, the English alphabet—with 26 letters—is pretty average. In comparison, the language with the longest alphabet in the world is the Cambodian language Khmer, boasting an impressive 74 letters. Rotokas, spoken in a small part of Papua New Guinea, has the shortest alphabet in the world with only 12 letters.

ACTIVITY

UNLEASH THE POWER OF CITRUS!

You're probably reeling after finding out so many riveting facts about the world we live in. Before you run off to share all this new information with anyone who will listen, it's time to watch natural wonders unfurl before your eyes in your very own home! In this easy yet engaging task, you'll get to see the magic that happens when you combine everyday ingredients lying around in your kitchen. You know what they say: When life gives you lemons, watch them erupt!

MATERIALS

- ↑ A lemon
- ← Liquid hand soap or dish soap
- ↑ Food coloring
- ↑ A large glass dish
- ↑ A teaspoon
- ↑ Baking soda
- ↑ A knife
- 🟢 Ask your parents for help!

INSTRUCTIONS

❶ Have your parents cut off the two ends of the lemon and then cut it in half, leaving two equal halves that have flat bottoms so they stay put.

❷ Place the lemon halves, with the wider part facing upward, inside the large glass dish. You can use a plate, but the dish ensures that we don't make a mess all over the kitchen and makes cleanup a lot easier!

❸ Pour a few drops of food coloring and a small amount of soap onto the exposed surface of each lemon half.

❹ Place a teaspoon of baking soda on top of the lemon halves. And now, watch in amazement! Your lemon halves will erupt like small acidic volcanoes into fizzy explosions of vibrant colors. To make the reaction bigger, use the teaspoon to push baking soda inside the lemons.

Totally Tectonic 111

Careful, the Robot May Byte

Engineering, technology and flying cars.

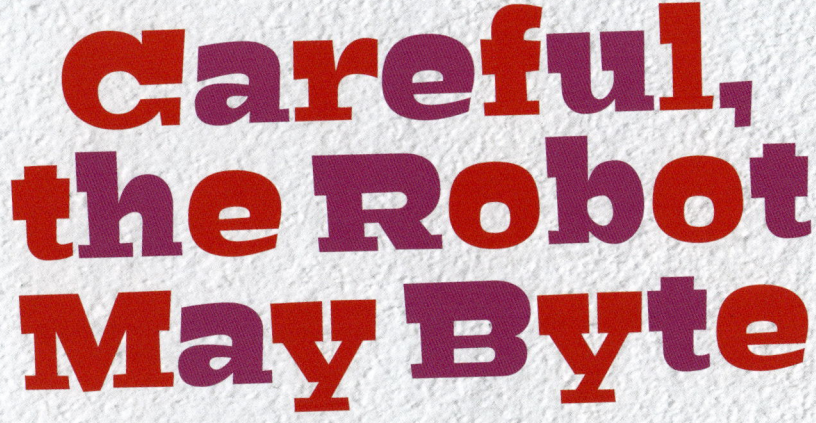

THIS IS A WHEELY GOOD IDEA!

The first cars did not have a steering wheel. Drivers changed directions using a lever for almost a decade until the handy steering wheel was invented in 1894!

A bionic eye that surpasses the capability of human vision has been developed. This device allows us to see ultraviolet and infrared light as well as visualize the polarization of light.

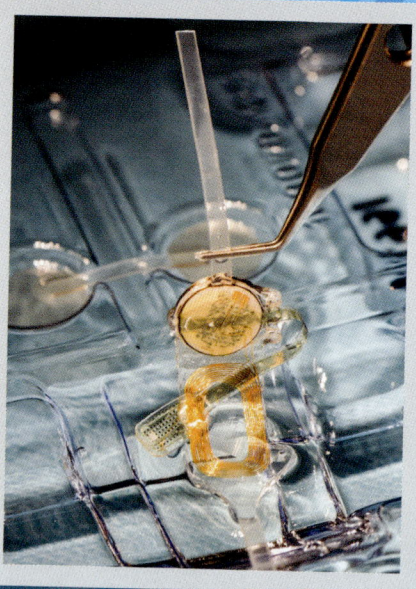

The fastest camera ever invented can capture as many as 10 trillion frames per second. This incredible feat of modern technology allows us to observe phenomena that are unbelievably fast, such as the movement of light!

Constructing buildings is difficult enough on Earth, so you can only imagine the challenges involved with building in space! The International Space Station was constructed over 10 years and took more than 30 missions into space to complete.

The U.S. National Weather Service reports that commercial aircraft are hit by lightning bolts once or twice a year on average. Luckily, advances in modern technology have ensured that it isn't hugely damaging to planes. In fact, no plane has crashed due to a lightning bolt hitting it since 1967, so all you need to worry about while flying is the bad airplane food!

The engines of electric cars are not only more environmentally friendly, they're also much simpler! Gas-powered engines typically have more than 2,000 moving parts, but electric engines only need around 20 to do the same job!

Electric cars were originally developed all the way back in the mid-1800s, before gasoline-powered cars! In 1859, prototypes with batteries that could be recharged came along, paving the way for the future. One of the reasons they are making such a comeback today is because of climate concerns.

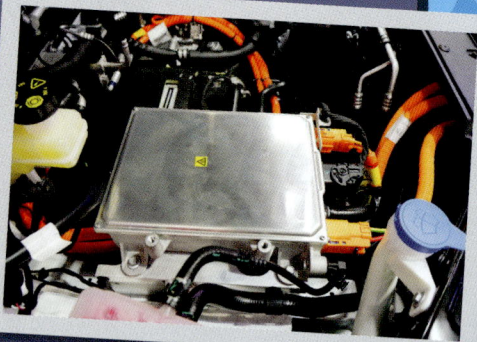

Did you know Nintendo existed long before computers? Founded in 1889, the company sold playing cards before video games were invented.

The Danyang-Kunshan Grand Bridge, located in China and finished in 2011 after four years of construction, is the longest bridge in the world. Its total length is 102.4 miles, and it cost roughly 8.5 billion in U.S. dollars to build!

A revolutionary robot named Atlas has such diverse mobility that it can do a backflip! The humanoid creation belongs to Boston Dynamics and aims to push the boundaries of robotic engineering, and are working to find ways to improve its already impressive parkour and gymnastic skills.

The very first analog computer was actually created 2,000 years ago! The Antikythera mechanism was a hand-powered device that helped ancient Greek civilizations predict the movements of stars and planets. However, the rapid advancement of digital computers is something that has only sped up in the last 20 years or so, ultimately leading us to the highly technical and fast-paced computers we use today.

Seeing a swaying building might ring alarm bells for some, but in the case of the CN Tower in Toronto, Canada, it's perfectly normal for this structure to sway up to 1.6 feet in high winds. It also gets struck by lightning about 75 times every year!

Flying cars are a feat of engineering often seen in futuristic sci-fi movies, but it may surprise you to learn that engineers have actually accomplished this seemingly impossible milestone. The AirCar is one such prototype currently in development, and was created in 2017 by Klein Vision. This astonishing invention transforms from a fully functional motor vehicle to an aircraft in 2 minutes and 15 seconds!

FASTEST!

The fastest speed for a car ever recorded is 763.035 miles per hour, a record set by the first vehicle to ever break the sound barrier! This speed was achieved back in 1997 by a jet-powered vehicle driven by Andy Green.

The greatest depth a person has ever traveled was 35,876 feet below the surface, a trip that took more than 4 hours of diving into the Challenger Deep—the deepest known section of the ocean. Believe it or not, there's some plastic litter down there!

Hailed as a marvel of geometry, engineering and biomechanics, the snowboard may seem like an ordinary object, but the specifics of this invention are actually highly calculated. It was invented by engineer **Sherman Poppen** in 1965. The design has evolved significantly over time, allowing snowboarders to perform more impressive tricks and become more aerodynamic.

BORED? TRY THIS!

TALLEST!

You may know the Ferris wheel as a fun theme park ride or a provider of great views, but this invention is actually a wonder of the engineering world. It was created by **George W. Ferris** in 1893. The wheel of the mechanism is supported by high steel towers and connected by a long, strong axle. The tallest one, the Ain Dubai, is located in Dubai and stands at 820 feet!

Invented in the twelfth century, the compass is a reliable piece of tech because it uses a magnetic field that runs between the North and South poles of our Earth to guide us. This also means a compass will continue to work if you go underground—the magnetic field is just as strong beneath the depths of the ocean or at the bottom of a mineshaft! However, because this magnetic field is maintained by the swirling molten iron at the core of our planet, you'd find that your compass would go crazy if you were ever able to dig that deep!

Frontier, the fastest supercomputer in the world, is used by the U.S. Department of Energy to perform scientific research. Frontier conducts more than 1.1 quintillion calculations every second! If every human in the world solved one math problem every second, it would still take us 4 years to complete the same amount of work that Frontier can produce in 1 second.

Standing at an impressive 305 feet tall, the Statue of Liberty, located in New York City, was given to the U.S. by its ally France in 1886. Back then, the statue was a shiny bronze color—but over time, the copper oxidized, giving the statue its signature light green hue.

THE GIFT THAT KEEPS ON GIVING!

While it sometimes refers to a fun dance move, the word "robot" actually has a dark hidden meaning. The word originally comes from the Czech word "robota," which means forced labor or work. First used to describe a machine in a play in the 1920s, the term simply stuck!

If it could only wake you up at 4 a.m., would you still want your alarm clock? Well, the very first one did exactly that. Invented in 1787 by Levi Hutchins, it would only sound off once, at 4 in the morning, every day! Luckily, in 1876, the wind-up alarm clock was invented, and the ringer could be set for any time.

Did you know that Google rented a herd of goats in place of lawnmowers? That's right—at their Mountain View headquarters in 2009, Google opted to rent 200 goats to eat the grass in place of mowing the lawns. It turned out to be such a good idea that nowadays you can easily find a goat to rent for gardening, too. No, I'm not kidding!

While reading from screens has undoubtedly become more popular, you might not want to give up your paperbacks just yet. Research has found that, on average, people read 10% slower on a screen than from paper! You also blink much less frequently when reading from a screen, which may cause your eyes to become dry and strained. So keep asking for books for the holidays!

Beneath the streets of Cincinnati, Ohio, lies an abandoned system of tunnels and train stations that has never been used. Approved for construction in the early 1900s to upgrade the streetcar system, work was interrupted by the First World War and eventually abandoned due to rising prices and political obstructions.

The tallest building in the world, the Burj Khalifa, is located in Dubai. It is a towering 2,717 feet tall, an astonishing height achieved through its unique design—it twists slightly as it goes higher, breaking up the wind at high altitudes so that it doesn't sway.

TALLEST!

One of the largest mosques in the world, the Sheikh Zayed Grand Mosque, is located in Abu Dhabi. It is supported by more than 1,000 pillars and has an incredibly luxurious interior. What may surprise you is that the most expensive part of this architectural marvel is the enormous carpet: it is, in fact, the largest handwoven carpet in the world! Thirty-eight tons of wool and cotton were used to make it, and it measures 60,568.5 square feet.

Have you ever been convinced you heard your phone buzz, but looked at the screen to see no new messages? This is a symptom of a very real condition called Phantom Vibration Syndrome. Research indicates this is caused by an over-dependence on cell phones. All the more reason to stick with books!

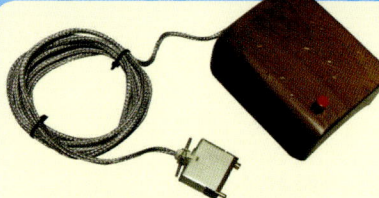

The first computer mouse was very different to the ones we use today. Doug Engelbart first stumbled upon this invention in 1964, only, back then, it was made from wood instead of plastic. He named it a "mouse" because the cord connecting it to the computer reminded him of a mouse's tail.

Would you ever consider a cell phone more essential than a toilet? Surprisingly, out of the world's 8.1 billion people, over 7 billion have access to a cell phone, while only 4.5 billion have a toilet at home.

The Eiffel Tower shrinks and grows depending on the temperature. Because it's made of iron, its height increases in hot weather when the iron expands, causing it to grow up to 15 centimeters taller than it is during the winter!

Some people have a phobia of technology. Named technophobia, this fear has roots going all the way back to the Industrial Revolution, when workers feared that new machines would take their jobs.

KNOW YOUR TOYS!

- When it was first invented, the humble hula hoop took the world by storm. First sold in 1958 by Wham-O, there were 25 million sales within its first four months on the market!

- Did you know there's a word for the study and science of puzzles? Enigmatology explores puzzles of any kind, whether related to math, words or logic.

- Founded in 1932 in Denmark, Lego is one of the most iconic toy brands that exists today. If you divided up the total number of Lego bricks sold, there would be enough for each person in the world to own an average of 86 bricks!

- The very first jigsaw puzzle was created in 1760, when John Spilsbury glued maps of the world onto wood and cut the wood into pieces. It was used to teach young children about geography and help them learn the location of different countries. These puzzles became popular and elite boarding schools began buying them.

KNOW YOUR TOYS! (CONTINUED)

- Your yo-yo may seem simple and unassuming, but it has a fascinating history as one of the oldest toys in the world! While its country of origin is undecided, with some saying it originated in China, the Philippines or Greece, there is undeniable evidence of its existence dating back to the year 500 B.C.

- Call her Barbie for short! Barbie, the most recognizable doll in the world, actually has a full name: Barbara Millicent Roberts! The name came from Barbie's original creator, Ruth Handler, who named the doll "Barbara" after her daughter.

- The fastest recorded time it took someone to solve a 3x3x3 rotating puzzle cube is 3.13 seconds! This incredible record was set in 2023 by the speedcubing giant and Guinness World Records Hall of Fame member Max Park, from the United States. He was only 21 years old!

- Crayola churns out nearly 3 billion crayons every year. That's enough crayons to circle our planet 6 times!

A family plays with the marble run at Adlerfelsen Mountain in Eibenstock, Germany, on July 7, 2016.

- The longest marble run was created on September 1st in Flumserberg, Switzerland, and measured 9,379.6 feet. However, the 4,638-foot marble run inside the Universum science facility in Bremen, Germany, set a world record for the longest running time, with their marble run of 36 minutes!

GET THE BALL ROLLING!

Has the wonderful world of technology and engineering enthralled you? While your brain is surely reeling after absorbing all that info, there's still more to come with this fun and challenging at-home activity. You'll be making your very own marble run—a fun-filled task for the whole family!

MATERIALS

➜ Marbles (or small balls)

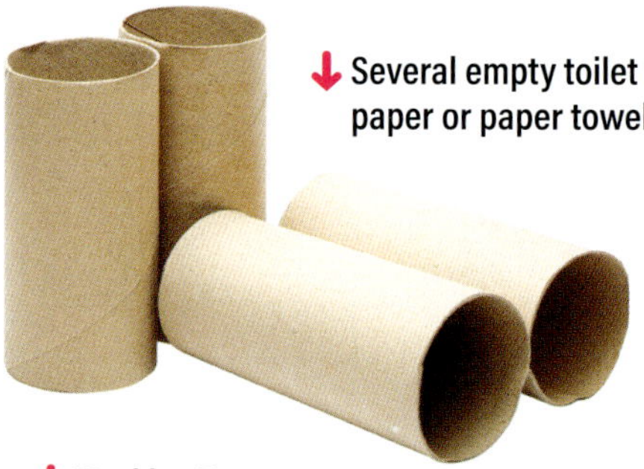

↓ Several empty toilet paper or paper towel rolls

↓ Masking Tape

INSTRUCTIONS

1 Find a wall that doesn't have anything hanging on it and use masking tape to attach the tubes to it. Make sure each tube is attached securely with multiple pieces of tape and that there are no gaps between where one tube ends and another begins. You don't want any marbles to fall out of the tunnel you're making! While this activity allows a lot of creative freedom, you'll also need to switch your engineering brain on to make sure the marble will flow through the tube design easily!

2 Place a box at the end so the marbles fall directly into it and don't tumble out all over the floor.

3 Once you're confident that your tunnel is securely attached to the wall and has no gaps, it's time to put it to the test! Pour your marbles into the entrance of the tunnel!

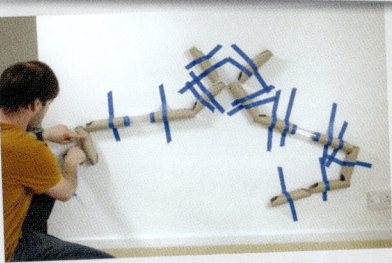
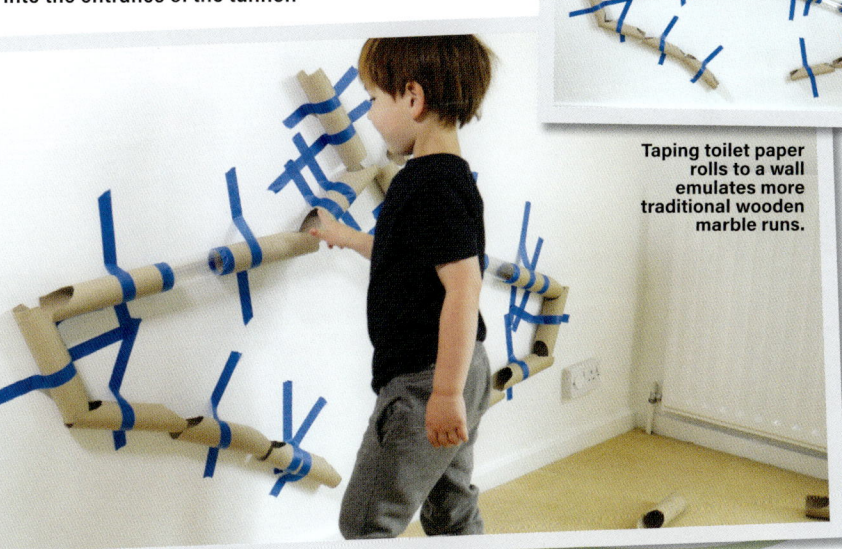

Taping toilet paper rolls to a wall emulates more traditional wooden marble runs.

TAKE IT FURTHER

Experiment with other materials for your marble run! It's fun to use a clear plastic sheet rolled up into a tube shape and attach it between two cardboard tubes. This way, at certain points, you can see your marbles rolling! Try using obstacles for the marbles as well as textured material to make their journey a little bumpier and more dynamic.

That Never Gets Old

History, origins and Viking tweezers.

Early humans first appeared in Africa and remained there for their first few million years. It was only about 1.8 million years ago that we began traveling to other parts of the world.

We are homo sapiens—the only surviving species of the genus Homo, the scientific name translating to "wise man" from Latin. It was first coined by Swedish botanist and taxonomist Carl Linnaeus.

A WISE MAN ONCE SAID...

Back when dinosaurs walked the earth, it actually rotated faster than it does today. This made days shorter, which meant dinos experienced 380 days in a year instead of our current 365!

5,000,000

The number of people on Earth has grown astronomically in quite a short amount of time. It is estimated that 5 million humans occupied the earth in 8000 B.C.—that's only about half the number of people currently living in London!

We weren't the only human species to inhabit Earth! We shared the same geographic areas with at least three other early human species. About 70,000 years ago, there were Denisovans, Homo floresiensis, and Homo neanderthalensis. The last of these—Homo neanderthalensis, commonly known today as the Neanderthals—is thought to have interbred with early Homo sapiens when the two species encountered one another, and this explains why recent genetic studies have found traces of Neanderthal DNA in most humans of non-African descent today.

Homo erectus, another species of early human, established itself as one of the longest-surviving human species to ever walk the earth! Existing for a period of time even greater than that of Homo sapiens, they are thought to have lived for about 1.8 million years. We've been around for a relatively short time in comparison—only 300,000 years!

Early Humans

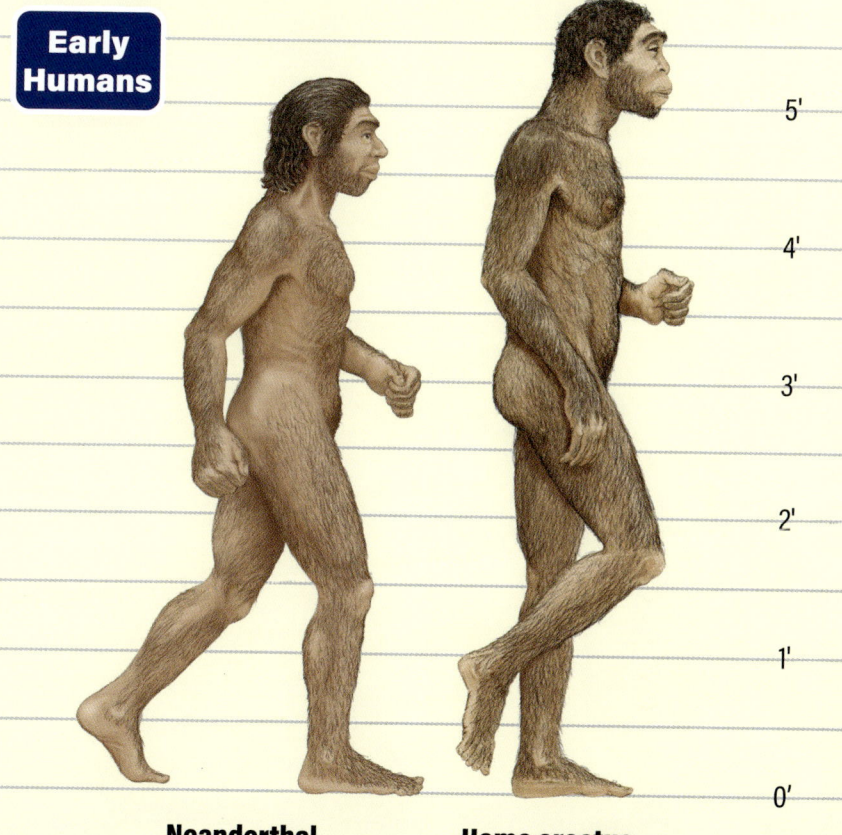

Neanderthal **Homo erectus**

That Never Gets Old

The T-rex is closer in history to us than to the stegosaurus! While we might think that all dinosaurs existed at the same time, this is far from the truth. The stegosaurus roamed the earth around 150 million years ago, while the Tyrannosaurus rex didn't even exist until only about 66 million years ago. That means there's an 84 million-year difference between the two dinosaur species. In fact, the T-rex is closer in history to us than to the stegosaurus!

Can you imagine watching the Olympic Games today if all the athletes performed their sports naked? Well, in the ancient Olympic Games, that's exactly what happened! This was a regular practice due to the belief that being naked helped bring them closer to the gods.

Olympic Games

Ever played tug-of-war? This fun and competitive game of strength was actually an official sporting event at the Olympic Games from 1900 to 1920! It was included in the track-and-field program!

The very first Olympic Games were held in the year 776 B.C., according to known records, and only one event was included—a footrace. Other events like wrestling, chariot racing, discus and jumping were added in later editions of the Games.

Did you know fine arts were once a part of the Olympic Games? That's right—from 1912 to 1952, gold medals were awarded in the categories of literature, architecture, music, painting and even sculpture! The art that was created had to be Olympic-themed.

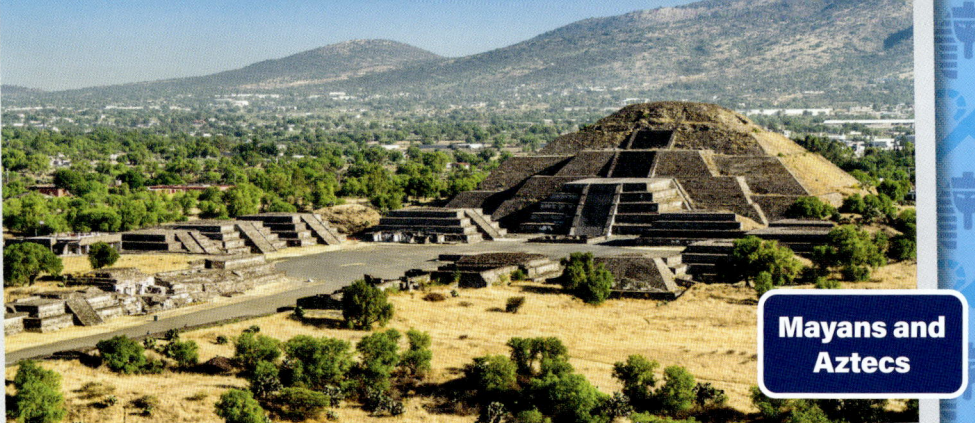

Mayans and Aztecs

We know the Aztec Empire is an ancient civilization, so it's pretty astonishing to think that the University of Oxford opened its doors almost 300 years before the Aztec Empire was founded! The institution began its monumental history of educating students back in 1096, while the Aztec Empire began with the building of its capital, Tenochtitlán, much later, in 1325.

Chocolate has been around for hundreds of years. The Mayans were already eating it back in the year 600 B.C.! They are believed to be the first civilization to mix cacao beans with water, honey, chili peppers and cornmeal to make a delicious early form of chocolate, according to an archaeological discovery in Belize that indicated residue from this mixture left on some very old ceramic molds.

While many believe the ancient Maya civilization simply disappeared overnight, this is actually untrue. This vibrant, sophisticated civilization existed from 1500 B.C. to A.D. 900 and experienced a gradual decline due to environmental changes, such as long droughts and deforestation. The civilization was also strained by overpopulation and warfare. But you can still meet Maya people today.

Alexander the Great, the ancient Greek king of Macedon, named more than 70 cities across the globe after himself. Alexandria in Egypt is arguably the most famous example, as it went on to become one of the most significant cultural hubs of the ancient Mediterranean world. He also named one city, Bucephala in Pakistan, after his horse, Bucephalus.

ALEX-CELLENT!

Elephants played an important role in Alexander the Great's conquests. These large mammals were used as medieval tanks, disrupting enemy formations and causing panic during battles.

With territories on every continent throughout the course of history, the British Empire is the largest empire the world has ever known. In 1919, it covered about 13.01 million square miles of land, which comes to about a quarter of the world's land!

Archaeological finds suggest that Vikings were conscious of personal hygiene. Ancient tweezers, razors, combs and even animal bones that were made into ear cleaners have been discovered. It is also believed that a special type of soap was created in Scandinavia and exported to other parts of the world, indicating that Vikings valued getting clean.

One of the world's greatest superpowers, the U.S.S.R., wasn't great for long. Also known as the Soviet Union, it was established in 1922, comprising 15 republics. It was also incredibly vast, spanning over one-sixth of the Earth's total land surface and covering 11 time zones. However, after political unrest and social reform, the superpower dissolved in 1991.

Tulips were once used as a form of currency in the Netherlands. During the 1630s, "Tulip Mania" erupted across the country and the flowers became incredibly valuable. Some bulbs even sold for the same value as a whole house! Dutch people would go so far as to trade their land, life savings and homes in exchange for tulip bulbs.

Hidden inside jars and tucked away in 11 caves surrounding the Dead Sea, the so-called Dead Sea Scrolls were discovered in 1947. The ancient texts were over 2,000 years old and included the earliest known copies of the Hebrew Bible, allowing us to learn a great deal about the past. On pg. 148, you too can create your own time capsule for people in the future to find.

For a brief period, the capital of Portugal was actually in Brazil. In 1808, following threats from Napoleon's armies during the Peninsular War, the Portuguese royal court left Europe and established themselves in Rio de Janeiro. It stayed that way for over a decade until the royal court returned to Lisbon in 1821. This was the only time in history when the capital of a European country was outside of Europe.

The Tsar Bomba was the largest nuclear bomb ever detonated. The Soviet Union set off this weapon of mass destruction in 1961 over the remote Arctic archipelago Novaya Zemlya. The intense blast equaled 3,000 times the power of the first atomic bomb, and the resulting shock wave circled the entire planet three times!

Did you know ketchup used to be sold as a common medicine? There were many varieties of ketchup made from many different kinds of things, including anchovies and oysters! As recently as the 1830s, these ketchups werebelieved to cure all kinds of ailments, including indigestion, jaundice and diarrhea! Ketchup was even sold in pill form.

I HAVE A BONE TO PICK WITH YOU, SIR...

The first dinosaur bone, discovered in 1677 by Robert Plot, was originally thought to belong to a giant human. William Buckland, the first geology professor at Oxford University, was the one who correctly identified this historic find as the bone of a long-deceased dinosaur.

Today, we associate the swastika with the violence and oppression exercised by the Nazi Party in Germany during the twentieth century. However, it was frequently used in many cultures over thousands of years, long before Adolf Hitler came into power. Ancient artifacts found in India, Greece, Rome and African regions display this symbol, which was previously associated with good luck, well-being and good fortune.

PHARAOH BEARDS AND INDESTRUCTIBLE HONEY

- Toothpaste has been around for many years. It was invented by the ancient Egyptians, who made the early version of this paste out of salt, pepper, mint and dried flowers. They considered white teeth to be a sign of health, beauty and youthfulness.

● Believe it or not, at the same time the pyramids were being built in Egypt, woolly mammoths were still roaming the earth! We have evidence suggesting mammoths were alive on a remote Arctic island until about the year 2000 B.C., and we know the Great Pyramid of Giza was assembled around 2560 B.C.

● Honey can never spoil. Indeed, archaeologists have discovered honey pots hidden in ancient Egyptian tombs that date back 3,000 years. The honey contained within is still perfectly edible!

● Did you know that when ancient Egyptians mummified people, they carefully removed and preserved the organs to keep them safe forever? However, since they believed that the heart was doing all the thinking, they threw the brain away!

That Never Gets Old

PHARAOH BEARDS AND INDESTRUCTIBLE HONEY (CONTINUED)

- Until the construction of Lincoln Cathedral in England in the fourteenth century, Egypt's Great Pyramid of Giza was hailed as the tallest structure built by man, a title it held for for more than 3,800 years!

- Having a beard in ancient Egypt was considered a sign of godliness, so pharaohs (even females) would often wear false ones tied to their chins with cords.

- Did you know Sudan has even more pyramids than Egypt? Several other countries are home to famous pyramids, including Mexico and Peru. However, with more than 200 pyramids, Sudan has the most of any country.

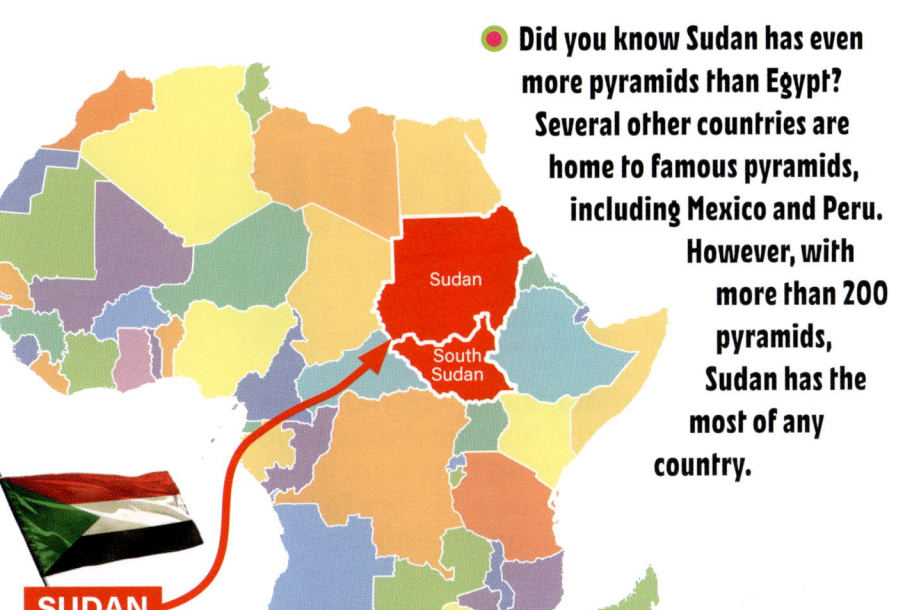

- The Rosetta Stone was discovered when Napoleon invaded Egypt. It was key to decoding ancient Egyptian hieroglyphics because the inscriptions on the Rosetta Stone say the same thing in three different scripts. Scholars could read the ancient Greek script and so were able to work out the meaning of hieroglyphs, too.

ACTIVITY

CREATE YOUR OWN TIME CAPSULE

Wow, who knew that history was hiding so many surprises? While the historical events you've just learned about occurred a long time ago, it's never too late to start recording your own history for people of the future to one day look back on. Creating a time capsule is a great activity to do together as a family—from finding and creating items to place in the capsule to setting an opening date that you all can look forward to and finally opening the capsule together someday in the future!

MATERIALS

- photographs
- coins
- small toys
- a map of your city or neighborhood
- your schoolwork or artwork
- stainless steel box or thick plastic container
- a newspaper and magazine

148 Fun Facts & Amazing Activities for Curious Kids

INSTRUCTIONS

1 It's important to choose a durable container as your time capsule. You'll want to use something that won't get easily damaged or break down over time. It is best to use a waterproof, airtight container. Your best option is either a stainless steel box or a thick plastic container. Consider adding an extra layer of protection like a resealable plastic bag.

2 Now it's time to select the items you want to put in your time capsule. Try to choose items you believe are significant to the present time and that people in the future may find interesting. As you select each item, discuss with one another why you believe it is significant or how it may be helpful to people of the future in understanding your current way of life.

3 As you go through the process of selecting items for the capsule, make predictions about how future generations may interpret these items.

4 When all the items have been gathered and placed into the capsule, have everyone in the group write a letter to the people who will one day uncover their items. You should include your hopes, thoughts and feelings about the present day and what you think the future may hold (even if you end up being the one to open the capsule!).

5 Now it's time to bury your capsule in a safe place. Make sure you seal it so that no air or water can penetrate the container and find a secure location to bury it. Make sure to somehow mark the spot where you've buried it so that you or other people can find it at a later date.

6 Finally, select a date when the capsule should be uncovered (if you want you and your family to be the ones to open it). This can be an important date, such as your 18th birthday or 20 years from today. This will give you all something to look forward to. One day, you can all come together again and celebrate the unearthing of the capsule!

Look at That Van Go!

Art, Yarn Bombing and Robot Rock Bands.

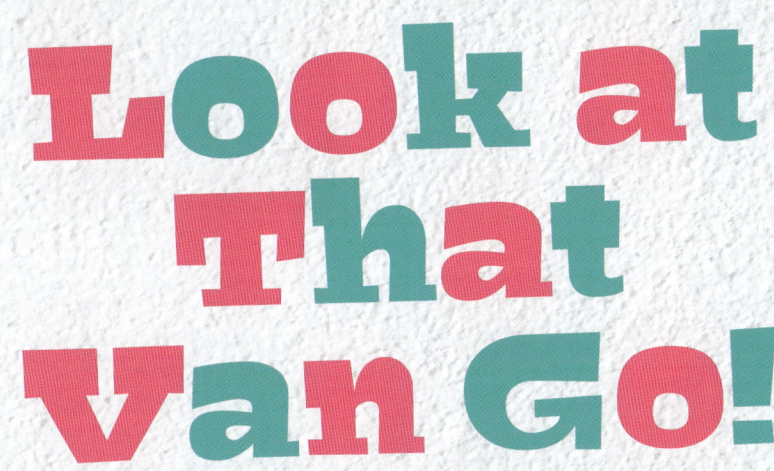

An unusual experiment conducted in Switzerland attempted to find out if exposing cheese to different types of music while it aged would impact its eventual flavor! The results determined that cheese exposed to hip-hop produced a stronger, fruitier flavor.

Did you know there's a band in which all the members are robots? It's called Compressorhead, and it fuses art and technology in a unique way. Animatronic robots were built from recycled parts and have been programmed to play real musical instruments! What sort of music do they play most often? You guessed it: heavy metal.

What's the smallest piece of art you've ever seen? Well, if you didn't need a microscope to view it, then it couldn't have been as small as the famous artworks painstakingly created by Willard Wigan. He creates sculptures so minute that they fit in the eye of a needle and viewers must look through a microscope to admire them. He once even accidentally inhaled a piece of a sculpture he was creating—Alice, from *Alice in Wonderland*! Luckily, the piece was remade even better the second time around.

The earliest known work of art was created more than 40,000 years ago! Cave paintings depicting pigs, horses and lions in what is now known as the Chauvet-Pont-d'Arc Cave in France are believed to have been painted by the Aurignacians, the earliest modern humans to occupy Europe.

It's sad to think about, but the world-famous and universally admired artist **Vincent van Gogh** sold only one painting in his lifetime. That one painting was sold for 400 francs in Brussels just a few months before the artist passed away. But in 2022, his painting *Orchard with Cypresses* sold for a record-breaking $117 million!

LEONARDO DA VINCI

One of the most well-known paintings in the world, the *Mona Lisa* wasn't famous until it was stolen from the Louvre in 1911. Vincenzo Peruggia, a museum worker, stole the painting with the intention of returning it to its home country of Italy. Leonardo da Vinci, who'd painted the Mona Lisa 350 years before the theft occurred, might have been happy to learn it was stolen—otherwise we might not care as much about it today!

Did you know that you can write letters to the *Mona Lisa*? The woman in the painting has her very own mailbox where admirers can send love letters, flowers and poems. Her mysterious smile has enchanted many over the years. The name of the painting translates to "My Lady Lisa," and the woman in the painting is thought to be Lisa Gherardini, a woman Leonardo da Vinci knew in Florence. So make sure you use her correct name to address her in your letter! You can mail it to:
Musée du Louvre,
Rue de Rivoli, 75001
Paris, France

Fun Facts & Amazing Activities for Curious Kids

There are actually four different versions of the famous painting *The Scream*. The artist, Edvard Munch, painted the original in 1893 and went on to create a pastel version later the same year. A third version was created and sold to a private buyer, and the fourth was given to the Munch Museum to be displayed to the public.

The color wheel was invented by **Isaac Newton** in 1666 by refracting pure white sunlight into six different colors. Today, the color wheel is used to describe colors accurately and illustrate relationships between colors, such as those opposite each other (called complementary). Variations of the wheel are often used by designers and artists!

COLOR ME INTRIGUED!

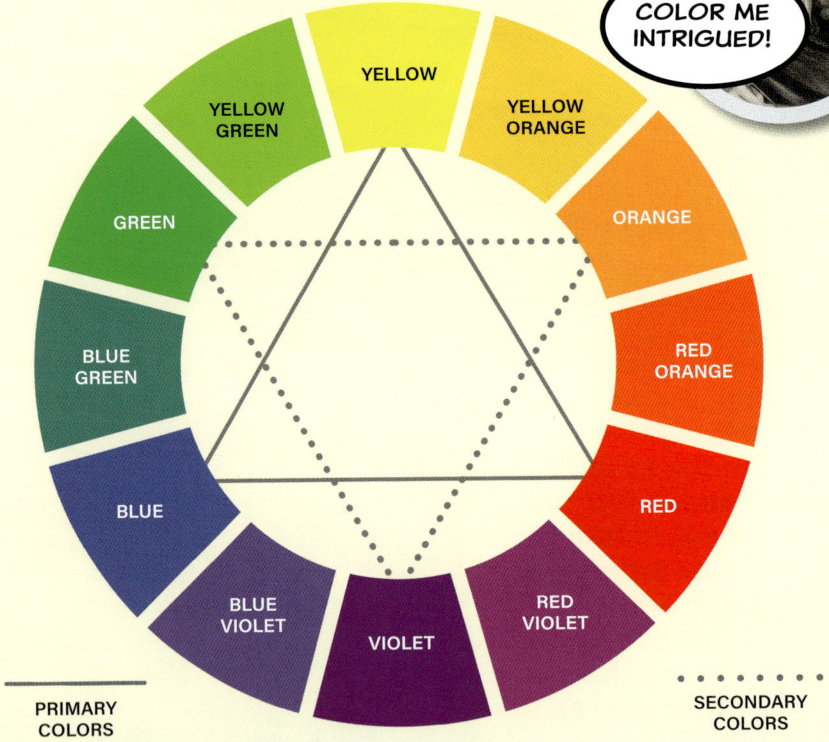

YELLOW
YELLOW GREEN
GREEN
BLUE GREEN
BLUE
BLUE VIOLET
VIOLET
RED VIOLET
RED
RED ORANGE
ORANGE
YELLOW ORANGE

PRIMARY COLORS

SECONDARY COLORS

156 Fun Facts & Amazing Activities for Curious Kids

"Prepared piano" is an innovative piano-playing technique invented by famous twentieth-century composer **John Cage**. Cage placed objects such as screws, pieces of kitchen foil and rubber ducks onto the strings of a piano and noted the new sounds that could be made when it was played. This astonishing technique allowed Cage to produce music no one had ever heard before!

THIS ONE'S IN THE KEY OF D, AS IN "DUCK."

Salvador Dalí believed for most of his life that he was the reincarnation of his older brother, also named Salvador, who died roughly nine months before his birth. He even featured images of his older brother in a few of his paintings, such as *Portrait of My Dead Brother*.

The oldest known musical composition is the Seikilos epitaph. It was found written on a column that formed a grave in Turkey, and it is believed to date back to the year A.D. 100. It includes lyrics and a musical score.

The peak of **Elvis Presley**'s musical career might have happened back in the 1950s and 1960s, but his popularity is still alive and well. With over 1 billion sales worldwide, the King of Rock & Roll is a Guinness World Record-holder for Best-Selling Solo Artist!

In August 2015, Canadian drummer Steve Gaul achieved the world record for the longest drumming marathon by an individual. He played for an astounding 134 hours and 5 minutes without stopping in order to raise money for charity.

As part of the London Palladium's Music is Magic concert in 2017, 1,521 triangle players performed together at the same time. Led by David Stanley and the Music Man Project, this magnificent collective is the largest triangle ensemble on record!

The Father of the Symphony, Austrian composer **Joseph Haydn**, strangely has two skulls in his tomb. While this may seem mysterious and slightly ominous, there's a good explanation. Someone actually broke into the tomb and stole his skull shortly after his death in 1809, so his family replaced it with a temporary one until the thief was caught. However, when the real skull was later recovered and returned to the tomb in 1954, the replacement skull remained.

LET'S PUT OUR HEADS TOGETHER AND THINK!

Wolfgang Amadeus Mozart is one of the most famous composers in history, but his sister was also incredibly talented. Maria Anna Mozart was known to play the piano equally as well as her gifted brother. Wolfgang and "Nannerl," as she was nicknamed, even played in multiple cities across Europe as child prodigies. However, Nannerl's career as a budding musician came to a close once she got a little older and married.

MANY HAVE SAID I PUT THE "ART" IN "MOZART."

Have you heard that listening to Mozart is believed to boost your brain's ability to solve complex puzzles? The "Mozart effect," first proposed in the 1990s, is a popular theory stating that listening to the composer's music regularly can improve a person's spatial-temporal abilities, allowing them to solve puzzles and reason with shapes more easily. While the publication of the theory originally boosted sales of Mozart's music, later research delivered a mix of results. Despite being unproven, the theory does make you think about the link between music and our mental capabilities.

Did you know that the famous composer **Ludwig van Beethoven** was almost entirely deaf by the time he reached his mid-40s? He began to lose his hearing in his late 20s, but despite this significant setback, he went on to compose some of his most iconic symphonies when he could barely hear at all. In fact, despite his deafness, he insisted that he conduct the opening premiere of his famous Symphony No. 9. Witnesses have said he continued conducting the orchestra after it had ceased playing, as he couldn't hear the audience applauding.

I AM VERY COMPOSED!

The phrase "don't play with your food" is widely disregarded by a unique musical group based in Vienna, Austria, known as the **Vegetable Orchestra**. They create compositions by playing instruments entirely made from vegetables such as carrots, pumpkins and peppers! And the fresh vegetables don't go to waste—after every performance, they are cooked into a vegetable soup, which the group shares with their audience.

The Sea Organ—located in Zadar, Croatia—is a uniquely built instrument that is played by the waves of the sea! This famous set of pipes is built into the steps of the coastline. Waves crashing up against it expel air through the pipes of the organ producing a range of musical sounds. These notes can be heard through holes made in the pavement, creating a harmonious symphony for everyone to enjoy.

Look at That Van Go!

Many musical composers have used non-traditional items, in addition to regular musical instruments, to add variety to their compositions. For example, David Lang used damaged instruments from public schools in Philadelphia for his piece *Symphony for a Broken Orchestra*. Sirens, anvils and a wind machine were used by Edgard Varèse in his piece *Ionization*, and George Crumb employed the use of crystal glasses and thimbles for his composition *Black Angels*.

Banksy is a famously mysterious artist known for his unique style. One of his paintings, *Girl with Balloon*, iconically self-destructed in 2018, mere moments after it was sold for a whopping £1 million ($1.4 million). The painting's frame was secretly fitted with a shredder that was activated remotely as soon as auction to acquire it ended. However, art experts estimate that the half-destroyed artwork has actually doubled in value since this public stunt.

The world's largest instrument is an organ located in Virginia's Luray Caverns. The Great Stalacpipe Organ covers about 161,459 square feet of the enormous cave and is made of rubber mallets that rhythmically tap icicle-shaped formations called stalactites that hang from the cave ceiling to produce musical notes.

There are several "musical roads" across the world that have been designed to create music when a car drives over them at a specific speed, such as "The Piano of Kilometer 1449" on National Route 237 in Argentina. As the wheels of a car move over grooves cut into the road's surface, they cause vibrations that produce tunes. You can hear the music from within the car as well as from the road, creating a highly unique driving experience!

Madhubani, a famous art style originating in Bihar, India, has helped decrease deforestation! Several artists gathered together in 2012 to create art pieces on the trunks of trees growing along a highway in the Madhubani district in an attempt to discourage people from chopping down the trees. It actually worked—not a single painted tree was destroyed! This area now attracts many tourists and brings awareness to the issue of deforestation.

Not only is art an essential form of self-expression and creativity, but it also contributes significantly to the economy. The worldwide art market was valued at more than $67.8 billion in 2022! This includes economic contributions from industries including painting, sculpture, photography and NFTs.

Yarn bombing, also known as guerrilla knitting or yarn graffiti, is a form of street art where artists cover public spaces with colorful knitted or crocheted yarn. Trees, lampposts and even statues become vibrant and cozy with these yarn installations.

Jan van Eyck's painting *The Arnolfini Portrait* displays its artist's reflection in a small mirror at the center of the canvas. In Rembrandt's famous painting *The Night Watch*, the artist actually features in the background of the painting—you can only see his eye and beret, but he's there!

Follow the instructions on the next page to create a deceptive work of art featuring your own hand.

ACTIVITY

TURN YOUR HAND INTO AN OPTICAL ILLUSION

It's time to let your inner artist shine through with a fun and engaging activity suitable for all ages. You can enjoy it by yourself or turn it into a family activity. Drawing a 3D image can look daunting and difficult, but this next challenge shows you how easy it can be.

MATERIALS

↑ A pencil

A piece of paper

↑ Your hand

↓ Any coloring materials (crayons, colored pencils, markers, etc.)

→ A ruler

INSTRUCTIONS

1 First, place your hand in the center of the paper and trace around it with a pencil.

2 Using a ruler, draw straight horizontal lines from one side of the paper to the other. Make sure not to allow the lines to cross over the outline of your hand—imagine your hand is at the front and the lines are behind it. The lines should be equal distance apart—about half an inch.

3 Draw curved lines inside your hand outline, with each curved line connecting to a straight line outside the hand outline. It might help to use your ruler, lining it up against each straight line one at a time. That way, you can see where the ends of each curved line need to connect to the corresponding straight line. The end result should be straight lines going across the page outside of the hand outline, with the lines appearing to curve "over" the hand outline.

4 Color each section created by the lines. Each line should be a different color. Try creating a pattern or just use a random color for each line. With a splash of color, you'll now start to see the illusion of your 3D hand coming to life!

TAKE IT FURTHER

For a more realistic 3D effect, try shading with a pencil along one side of the hand and fingers. You can use this technique to turn other objects into 3D illusions too.

AFTERWORD

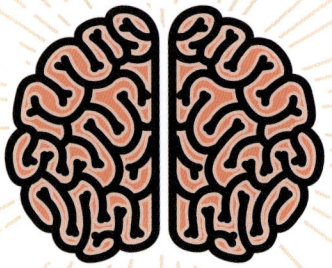

IT'S A WRAP, BRAIN-WAVERS! BUT WE'VE ONLY SCRATCHED THE SURFACE...

Well, my friend, here you are at the end of the book, but only at the beginning of an extraordinary journey of discovery that I hope it's inspired.

Our expedition began as a quest for fun, and oh boy, I hope you had plenty of it! But if you take one thing from this book, let it be that we are never done learning. Even though you have just gobbled up an astounding array of facts, the universe remains an infinite buffet of knowledge waiting for you to sample! There are always more questions to be asked, more phenomena to observe and more places in time and space to explore. The knowledge you can acquire truly has no limits!

So, I challenge you to keep exploring and keep having fun. After all, the greatest adventures begin with a single spark of curiosity.

Thank you for joining me on this adventure. I hope it's been as thrilling for you as it has for me, and I'm excited to see where your newfound knowledge leads you.

By the way, did you figure out the hidden message via the red letters scattered throughout the book?

ANSWER:

CURIOSITY LEADS TO DISCOVERY (printed upside down)

BUT WAIT, THERE'S MORE!

I'm inviting you to join the fact-hunting party! If you stumble upon a fact so cool it makes your eyebrows shoot up, I'd love to hear it, and so would the rest of TheDadLab community!

Submit your facts to www.thedadlab.com/facts or share them on social media by tagging @thedadlab and using the hashtag #thedadlab Because when it comes to learning, the more the merrier!

Keep exploring,

Scan and share your amazing facts!

PHOTO CREDITS

COVER: background: OHishi_Foto/AdobeStock; earth: banphote/AdobeStock; kid: Shutterstock; giraffe: Buse/AdobeStock; tube: SDF_QWE/AdobeStock; astronaut: fStop Images GmbH/Alamy; astronaut hose: colematt/iStock; moon: ismailbasdasAdobeStock; robot: Optinik/AdobeStock; math formula: SupakornAng/AdobeStock; pyramids: Ahmed/AdobeStock
BACK COVER: background: Olexandr/AdobeStock; marbles: dule964/AdobeStock; dinosaur: Giama22/AdobeStock; Eiffel Tower: Photobeps/AdobeStock; comet: Tryfonov/AdobeStock
INTERIOR: 5 clockwise from top left: Wolfilser/AdobeStock; egorxfi/AdobeStock; 3dsculptor/AdobeStock; Hayati Kayhan/AdobeStock; lloyd fudge/AdobeStock; LademannMedia/Alamy; ILYA AKINSHIN/AdobeStock; nerthuz/AdobeStock; B. Barrett/Maine Mineral and Gem Museum; Jut/AdobeStock 6-7 background: Maximusdn/AdobeStock; earth: TOimages/AdobeStock; Elvis: RGR Collection/Alamy; retro rocket: charles taylor/AdobeStock; Mona Lisa: Dennis MacDonald/Alamy; nickel: BillionPhotos.com/AdobeStock; rubik's cube: DGTL Graphics sro/AdobeStock; Statue of Liberty: Brad Pict/AdobeStock; woolly mammoth: noman/AdobeStock; 8 clockwise from left: zcy/AdobeStock; Rafael Ben-Ari/AdobeStock; Maximusdn/AdobeStock; 9 Courtesy of Sergei Urban; 10-11 background top to bottom: Gabriele Maltinti/AdobeStock; MaciejBledowski/AdobeStock; icemanphotos/AdobeStock (2); Aura/AdobeStock; giraffe: Buse/AdobeStock; tube: SDF_QWE/AdobeStock; sun: Günter Albers/AdobeStock; clouds: NeoLeo/AdobeStock; ParinPIX/AdobeStock; 12-13 clockwise from top left: nsit0108/AdobeStock; rufar/AdobeStock; vladimirfloyd/AdobeStock; BNP Design Studio/AdobeStock; Good Studio/AdobeStock; 14-15 clockwise from top left: tigatelu/AdobeStock; jacartoon/AdobeStock; FotoHelin/AdobeStock; Mark Kostich/AdobeStock; 16-17 clockwise from top left: BillionPhotos.com/AdobeStock; VALERIA TARLEVA/AdobeStock; iulianvalentin/AdobeStock; Pixel-Shot/AdobeStock; nikolaynachkov/AdobeStock; 18-19 clockwise from top left: Jayce Giddens/AdobeStock; Barudak Lier/AdobeStock; SVIATOSLAV/AdobeStock; Vasyl Helevachuk/AdobeStock; wen/AdobeStock; 20-21 clockwise from top left: brgfx/AdobeStock; Konstantin Postumitenko/AdobeStock; Dadan/AdobeStock; AlbyDeTweede/iStock; Віталій Баріда/AdobeStock; rawinfoto/AdobeStock; 22-23 clockwise from top left: Solvin Zankl/NPL/Minden Pictures; Papilio/Alamy; nenilkime/AdobeStock; Premaphotos/Alamy; Andrea Izzotti/AdobeStock; 24-25 clockwise from top left: Dustin Barnett/Wirestock/AdobeStock; Gerald Robert Fischer/AdobeStock; Anja Hennern/AdobeStock; Ash/AdobeStock; Francesco/AdobeStock; Adisha Pramod/Alamy; 26-27 clockwise from top left: Baiba Opule/AdobeStock; nechaevkon/AdobeStock; Andrey Kuzmin/AdobeStock; Judith Dueck/AdobeStock; Reto Ammann/AdobeStock; Farinoza/AdobeStock; 28-29 clockwise from top left: hiv360/AdobeStock; leungchopan/AdobeStock; Igor Dmitriev/AdobeStock; Gerard LACZ/AdobeStock; bullet_chained/AdobeStock; 30-31 clockwise from top left: jasonyu/AdobeStock; Chris/AdobeStock; ILYA AKINSHIN/AdobeStock; Yinzhong/AdobeStock; Vector Tradition/AdobeStock; 32-33 clockwise from top left: Victor Moussa/AdobeStock; Yukihiro Kawauchi/AdobeStock; photosvac/AdobeStock; Harry Collins/AdobeStock; Cavan Images/AdobeStock; 34 clockwise from top: Aleksandr Shyripa/AdobeStock; pamela_d_mcadams/AdobeStock; Andrei Kuzmik/AdobeStock; Coprid/AdobeStock; 35 deagreez/AdobeStock; 36-37 tablecloth: Gray wall studio/AdobeStock; napkins: bigacis/AdobeStock; silverware: grey/AdobeStock; plate: The Big L/AdobeStock; pizza: Rustam/AdobeStock; 38-39 left to right: Marco Govel/AdobeStock; Anthony Hargreaves/AdobeStock; JetHuynh/AdobeStock; sabelskaya/AdobeStock; 40-41 clockwise from top left: Science History Images/Alamy; Frogella.stock/AdobeStock; Cheryl Graham/Wikipedia.org; 42-43 clockwise from top left: Krzysztof Bubel/AdobeStock; jackhollingsworth.com/AdobeStock; netsign/AdobeStock; Fotofermer/AdobeStock; bychykhin/AdobeStock; 44-45 clockwise from left: sudowoodo/AdobeStock; Vladyslav/AdobeStock; New Africa/AdobeStock; 46-47 clockwise from top left: tydeline/AdobeStock; Suradech/AdobeStock; Екатерина Якубович/AdobeStock; 48-49 clockwise from top left: ahmetcigsar/AdobeStock; sila5775/AdobeStock; MMphotos/AdobeStock; Kaspars Grinvalds/AdobeStock; 50-51 clockwise from top left: Pink Badger/AdobeStock; Casther/AdobeStock; prostoira777/AdobeStock; Mariusz Blach/AdobeStock; Anthony Hargreaves/AdobeStock; 52-53 crayons: chas53/AdobeStock; map: tortugin/AdobeStock; paper sheets: onephoto/AdobeStock; pencil: Vitaly Zorkin/AdobeStock; eraser: photomelon/AdobeStock; boy: Asier/AdobeStock; 54-55 sky: candy1812/AdobeStock; girl: Blue_Cutler/iStock; red balloon bottom left: martanfoto/AdobeStock; all other balloons: Oleksandr Dibrova/AdobeStock; bird: uha Saastamoinen/AdobeStock; 56-57 clockwise from top left: Optinik/AdobeStock; Hein Nouwens/AdobeStock; Krupal/AdobeStock; Uwe Bergwitz/AdobeStock; mode_list/AdobeStock; 58-59 clockwise from top left: BillionPhotos.com/AdobeStock; kolonko/AdobeStock; diy13/AdobeStock; Clerence/AdobeStock; Retouch man/AdobeStock; 60-61 clockwise from top left: denis08131/AdobeStock; Jemastock/AdobeStock; nchamunee/AdobeStock; shaiith/AdobeStock; arvitalya/AdobeStock; Fotoskat/AdobeStock; 62-63 clockwise from top left: Christopher Hall/AdobeStock; Artsiom P/AdobeStock; tigatelu/AdobeStock; unpict/AdobeStock (2); savage ultralight/AdobeStock; 64-65 from left: Ekky/AdobeStock; New Africa/AdobeStock; Adrien/AdobeStock; 66-67 clockwise from top left: TOimages/AdobeStock; kolonko/AdobeStock; juliedeshaies/AdobeStock; Archive PL/Alamy; master1305/AdobeStock; 68-69 clockwise from top left: elements: kolonko/AdobeStock; totojang1977/AdobeStock; MoreVector/AdobeStock; 70-71 clockwise from top left: grey/AdobeStock; Steve Cukrov/AdobeStock; fifg/AdobeStock; Coprid/AdobeStock; elements: kolonko/AdobeStock; 72 clockwise from left: Александр Трубицын/AdobeStock; natatravel/AdobeStock; Kimberly Reinick/AdobeStock; Maksim/AdobeStock; 73 row 1: slawek_zelasko/AdobeStock; sommai/AdobeStock; Kuzmick/AdobeStock; Da-ga/AdobeStock; row 2: dule964/AdobeStock; Coprid/AdobeStock; StockPhotosArt/AdobeStock; row 3: leventina/AdobeStock; Olha/AdobeStock; saneh/AdobeStock; row 4: grey/AdobeStock; lena_zajchikova/AdobeStock; 74-75 clockwise from left: lekcej/iStock; Sara Sadler/Alamy (2); Ian_Redding/iStock; 76-77 background: arvitalya/AdobeStock; astronaut left: bbtree/Alamy; astronaut right: Delphotostock/AdobeStock; saturn: Richard/AdobeStock; earth: 1xpert/AdobeStock; rocket: bramgino/AdobeStock; moon: Martin/AdobeStock; golf ball: Galina/AdobeStock; 78-79 clockwise from top left: Magnascan/iStock; Leonid Ikan/AdobeStock; Paolo Gallo/AdobeStock; Turner, O. J/Library of Congress; 80-81 clockwise from top left: magann/AdobeStock; kolonko/AdobeStock; Tristan3D/AdobeStock; bescec/AdobeStock; 82-83 clockwise from top left:Johnson Space Center/NASA; Natalia/AdobeStock; Tashi-Delek/iStock; Andrii Vergeles/AdobeStock; D1min/AdobeStock; 84-85 clockwise from top left: Olesia_g/AdobeStock; Jonas Weinitschke/AdobeStock; IanDagnall Computing/Alamy; Leonid Tit/AdobeStock; 86-87 clockwise from top left: vladischern/AdobeStock; planets: Nadzin/AdobeStock; passmil198216/AdobeStock; Alexey Kuznetsov/AdobeStock; 88 roman figures: matiasdelcarmine/AdobeStock (5); mars: Good Studio/AdobeStock; solar system: blueringmedia/AdobeStock; 89 from top: Science Photo Library/Alamy; JSirlin/AdobeStock; M/AdobeStock; 90-91 clockwise from top left: SashaMagic/AdobeStock; Romolo Tavani/AdobeStock; Muhammad/AdobeStock; Johnson Space Center/NASA; 92 girl:Quality Stock Arts/AdobeStock; rubber band:pixelrobot/AdobeStock; straw: koosen/AdobeStock; car: Dorling Kindersley ltd/Alamy; balloon: aperturesound/AdobeStock; 93 from top: Dorling Kindersley ltd/Alamy; Rob hyrons/AdobeStock; Dorling Kindersley ltd/Alamy; 94-95 background: gluuker/AdobeStock; eiffel tower: Photobeps/AdobeStock; Big Ben: sborisov/AdobeStock; boy: rostock-studio/AdobeStock; globe: cnky photography /AdobeStock; volcano: Scheidle-Design/AdobeStock; temple: chalermphon/AdobeStock; 96-97 clockwise from top left: grgroup/AdobeStock; Duncan Andison/AdobeStock; BooblGum/AdobeStock; B. Barrett/Maine Mineral and Gem Museum; 98-99 clockwise from top left: lesniewski/AdobeStock; Adrian Wojcik/Alamy; Naeblys/AdobeStock; 100-101 clockwise from top left: Tatiana Gasich/AdobeStock; MINIWIDE/AdobeStock; Geng Xu/iStock; Kooh Studio/AdobeStock; Richie Chan/AdobeStock; 102-103 clockwise from top left: Netfalls/AdobeStock; bogdanserban/AdobeStock; infinity/AdobeStock; soleilc1/AdobeStock; Claudio Divizia/AdobeStock; 104-105 clockwise from left: SeanPavonePhoto/AdobeStock; Karim Bouchetata/Alamy; Claudio Divizia/AdobeStock; Artalis-Kartographie/AdobeStock; 106-107 clockwise from top left: vectortatu/AdobeStock; PB/YB/Alamy; a_medvedkov/AdobeStock; Dimitrios/AdobeStock; 108-109 clockwise from left: FatCamera/iStock; Kevin/AdobeStock; Peter Hermes Furian/AdobeStock; Adil/AdobeStock; railwayfx/AdobeStock; 110 clockwise from top left: seralex/AdobeStock; chones/AdobeStock; pamela_d_mcadams/AdobeStock; BillionPhotos.com/AdobeStock; buki77/AdobeStock; framarzo/AdobeStock; dule964/AdobeStock; 111 AntonioDiaz/AdobeStock; inset: Science History Images/Alamy; 112-113 background: wcirco; ferris wheel: Zahreen; Statue of Liberty: Wirestock/iStock; building: FevreDream/iStock; car: OlegMirabo; wings: Sentavio/AdobeStock; robot: Josh Reynolds/AP images; 114-115 clockwise from top left: Sueddeutsche Zeitung Photo/Alamy; artbalitskiy/AdobeStock; Johnson Space Center/NASA; Phanie - Sipa Press/Alamy; 116-117 clockwise from top left: KawiGirl06/AdobeStock; Tim Whitby/Alamy; Imaginechina Limited/Alamy; Aflo Co. Ltd./Alamy; Supersmario/iStock; Mike Mareen/AdobeStock; 118-119 clockwise from top left: Ancient Art and Architecture/Alamy; Mocsonoky Peter/AdobeStock; PA Images/Alamy; ratpack223/AdobeStock; Xinhua/Alamy; 120-121 clockwise from top left: Sherman Poppen Papers, Archives Center, National Museum of American History, Smithsonian Institution; BillionPhotos.com/AdobeStock; Brad Pict/AdobeStock; creativefamily/AdobeStock; History and Art Collection/Alamy; snowboard: Colorado Snowsports Museum and Hall of Fame; 122-123 clockwise from top left: charles taylor/AdobeStock; Odua Images/AdobeStock; dblight/iStock; Igor Zakowski/AdobeStock; MET/BOT/Alamy; 124-125 clockwise from top left: Mazur Travel/AdobeStock; phone: wasan/AdobeStock; scale: jroballo/AdobeStock; toilet: Poprock3d/AdobeStock; Photobeps/AdobeStock; aldomurillo/iStock; dpa picture alliance/Alamy; 126-127 clockwise from left: kali9/iStock; Юлия Васильева/AdobeStock; zcy/AdobeStock; Christie's Images/Bridgeman Images; 128-129 clockwise from top left: kateleigh/AdobeStock; Piero Oliosi/Polaris/Newscom; BillionPhotos.com/AdobeStock; dpa picture alliance/Alamy; DGTL Graphics sro/AdobeStock; 130 marbles top: photomelon/AdobeStock; marbles center: THP Creative/AdobeStock; toilet paper rolls: prasith/Adobe/Stock; tape: MONTRI/AdobeStock; boy: KAMPUS/AdobeStock; 131 Courtesy of Sergei Urban; 132-133 pyramid: frenta/AdobeStock; greek columns: Ievgen Skrypko/AdobeStock; caveman: Roni/AdobeStock; viking ship: koya979/AdobeStock; tulips: firewings/AdobeStock; flame: marina_ua/AdobeStock; ground: zhu difeng/AdobeStock; ocean waves top to bottom: fotoliasc2014/AdobeStock; vectorfusionart/AdobeStock; Youk/AdobeStock; 134-135 clockwise from top left: IanDagnall Computing/Alamy; Universal Images Group North America LLC/Alamy (2); Comauthor/AdobeStock; 136-137 clockwise from top left: Penta Springs Limited/Alamy; Nicholas Felix/peopleimages.com/AdobeStock; alexus/AdobeStock; Sonulkaster/AdobeStock; PatternHousePk/AdobeStock; pascal/AdobeStock; 138-139 clockwise from top left: Leonid Andronov/AdobeStock; MidoSemsem/AdobeStock; Anton Starikov/Alamy; Cavan Images/Alamy; Franciane Souza/AdobeStock; 140 PRISMA ARCHIVO/Alamy; 141 Micha Klootwijk/AdobeStock; Olena Znak/AdobeStock; 142-143 clockwise from top left: vadiml/AdobeStock; WP!/AdobeStock; Science History Images/Alamy; Micha Klootwij/Alamy; Album/Alamy; 144-145 clockwise from top left: Віталій Баріда/AdobeStock; noman/AdobeStock; Olesia/AdobeStock; Jose Ignacio Soto/AdobeStock; BillionPhotos.com/AdobeStock; K. A./peopleimages.com/AdobeStock; 146-147 clockwise from top left: Pius Lee/AdobeStock; cloudvisual/AdobeStock; Dancing Man/AdobeStock; Peter Hermes Furian/AdobeStock; Özgür Güvenç/AdobeStock; Jose Ignacio Soto/AdobeStock; 148 clockwise from top left: Syda Productions/AdobeStock; REDPIXEL/AdobeStock; Denise Torres/AdobeStock; ksena32/AdobeStock; Kittiphan/AdobeStock; voraphong pirawd/AdobeStock; AlenKadr/AdobeStock; BillionPhotos.com/AdobeStock; homeworks255/iStock; center: czarny_bez/AdobeStock; 149 BNP Design Studio/AdobeStock; 150-151 Van Gogh: Charlie J Ercilla/Alamy; Mona Lisa: Dennis MacDonald / Alamy; Elvis: PictureLux / The Hollywood Archive/Alamy; Beethoven: visuals-and-concepts/AdobeStock; bike: Malin Quintern/Alamy; rock painting: Nature Picture Library/Alamy; music notes: Khai/AdobeStock; 152-153 clockwise from top left: Jakkarin 14/AdobeStock; sewonboy/Adobestock; LademannMedia/Alamy; Nature Picture Library/Alamy; sforzza/AdobeStock; PA Images/Alamy; 154-155 clockwise from top left: Photo 12/Alamy; claraveritas/Adobestock; mustafavarlik/Adobestock; N.Savranska/Adobestock; background: Blickfang/AdobeStock; 156 clockwise from top left: Antiquarian Images/Alamy; Archivist/AdobeStock; Nattaya/AdobeStock; 157 top right: United Archives GmbH/Alamy; tin foil: Savvapanf Photo/AdobeStock; duck: Andrzej Tokarski/AdobeStock; screws: medwedja/AdobeStock; bottom: Keystone Press/Alamy; 158-159 clockwise from top left: United Archives GmbH/Alamy; Kristians Berents/Wirestock/AdobeStock; Archivist/AdobeStock; Kitypaws design/AdobeStock; Mathias Weil/AdobeStock; 160-161 clockwise from top left: North Wind Picture Archives/Alamy; dpa picture alliance/Alamy; borongich/AdobeStock; visuals-and-concepts/AdobeStock; MNStudio/AdobeStock; vegetables: NASYUKA/AdobeStock; 162-163 clockwise from top left: onzon/AdobeStock; chrisstockphoto/Alamy; annacovic/AdobeStock; Alexandre Tziripouloff/Alamy; Graficriver/AdobeStock; Mustafa/AdobeStock; BillionPhotos.com/AdobeStock; koya979/AdobeStock; 164-165 clockwise from top left: RealityImages/AdobeStock; Alvaro German Vilela/Alamy; IanDagnall Computing/Alamy; Album/Alamy; Wahyu/AdobeStock; 166 hand: sinseeho/AdobeStock; pencil: chones/AdobeStock; ruler: PrimeMockup/AdobeStock; paper: POKPAK/AdobeStock; colored pencils: vladographer/AdobeStock; 167: from top: Seventyfour/AdobeStock; gilbe522 / Stockimo/Alamy; 168-169 grgroup/AdobeStock; Colorfuel Studio/AdobeStock; 170-171 skynesher/iStock

ACKNOWLEDGMENTS

First and foremost, a shoutout to all curious minds out there. Keep those questions coming! Let's never stop being amazed by the world around us. A big thank you to YOU, my reader!

Thank you to my children, my fearless lab assistants and partners in mess-making. Thanks for enduring my occasional explosive experiments and for asking "Why?" a million times. You're the reason I do what I do.

To my amazing wife, Tania, who's not only my better half but also the patient one. You're my anchor in this whirlwind.

To all the animals, plants, rocks and stars that make our world a mind-blowing place: Your odd behaviors, complex ecosystems and strange phenomena are the reason we have a book full of wild facts to begin with.

To all the science teachers who ignite the spark of curiosity in us, thank you. You show us that science is an adventure waiting to happen. I hope this book captures a fraction of the enthusiasm you instill in us.

To my neighbors, who kindly pretended not to notice the strange noises, occasional bangs and mysterious glowing coming from our house. We promise we're not building a doomsday device—just trying to figure out how to make the best slime!

To my literary agent, Kathleen Ortiz, the keeper of my wild ideas. Thank you for putting up with my creative chaos and supporting me through it all. You're the true mastermind behind the madness.

And finally, to my co-conspirator in this fact-finding frenzy, my editor, Beth Eynon. Thank you for joining me on this wild ride. Who knew that our shared curiosity and a good laugh could lead to a book?

With endless curiosity and gratitude,

Sergei Urban

Media Lab Books
For inquiries, contact customerservice@topixmedia.com

Copyright © 2024 U-Studio Ltd

PUBLISHED BY TOPIX MEDIA LAB
14 WALL STREET, SUITE 3C
NEW YORK, NY 10005

PRINTED IN CHINA

All rights reserved. No part of this book may be reproduced in any form or by any electronic or mechanical means, including information storage and retrieval systems, without permission in writing from the publisher, except by a reviewer, who may quote brief passages in a review.

The information in this book has been carefully researched, and every reasonable effort has been made to ensure its accuracy. Neither the book's publisher nor its creators assume any responsibility for any accidents, injuries, losses or other damages that might come from its use. You are solely responsible for taking any and all reasonable and necessary precautions when performing the activities detailed in its pages.

Certain artwork used in this publication is used by license or permission from the owner thereof or is otherwise publicly available. This publication is not endorsed by any person or entity appearing herein. Any product names, logos, brands or trademarks featured or referred to in the publication are the property of their respective trademark owners. Media Lab Books is not affiliated with, nor sponsored or endorsed by, any of the persons, entities, product names, logos, brands or other trademarks featured or referred to in any of its publications.

ISBN-13: 978-1-956403-99-2
ISBN-10: 1-956403-99-X

CEO Tony Romando

Vice President & Publisher Phil Sexton
Senior Vice President of Sales & New Markets Tom Mifsud
Vice President of Retail Sales & Logistics Linda Greenblatt
Vice President of Manufacturing & Distribution Nancy Puskuldjian
Digital Marketing & Strategy Manager Elyse Gregov
Chief Content Officer Jeff Ashworth
Senior Acquisitions Editor Noreen Henson
Creative Director Susan Dazzo
Photo Director Dave Weiss
Executive Editor Tim Baker
Managing Editor Tara Sherman

Content Designer Mikio Sakai
Content Editor Trevor Courneen
Associate Editor Juliana Sharaf
Designers Glen Karpowich, Alyssa Bredin Quirós
Copy Editor & Fact Checker Madeline Raynor
Assistant Photo Editor Jenna Addesso
Assistant Managing Editor Claudia Acevedo

1C-G24-1

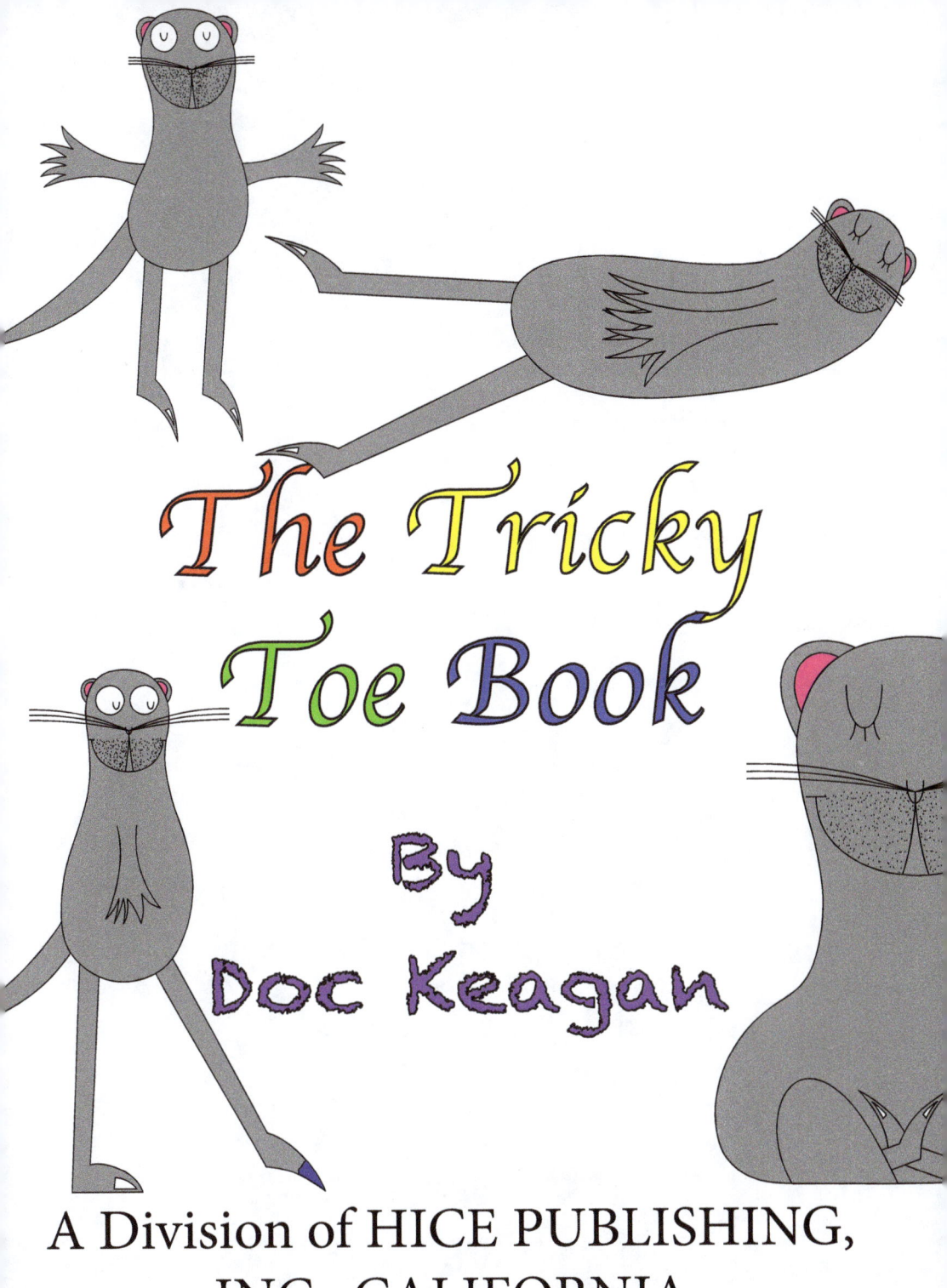

The Tricky Toe Book

By Doc Keagan

A Division of HICE PUBLISHING, INC., CALIFORNIA
Unique Learner Books

The mustelid has criss-cross toes.

The mustelid has tippy toes.

The mustelid has sleeping toes.

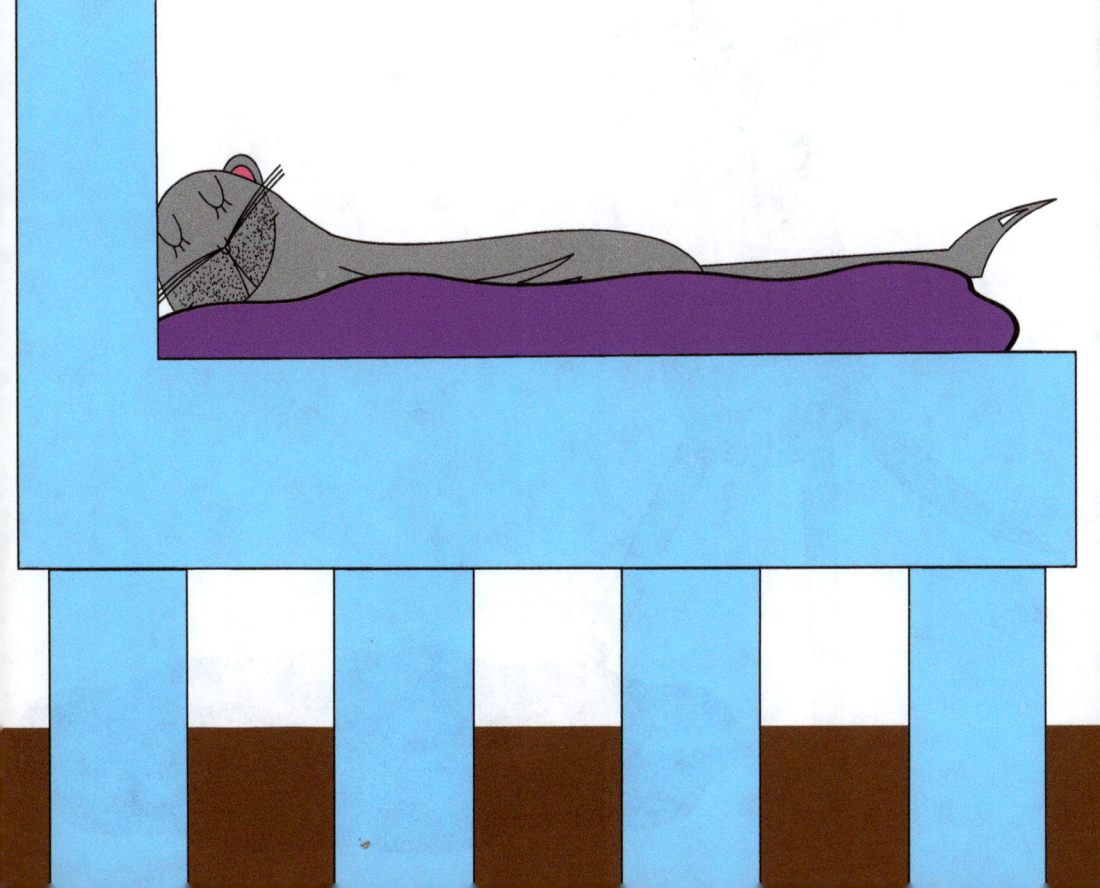

The mustelid has dipping toes.

The fancy girl has painting toes.
Her painted toes are vibranty pink!

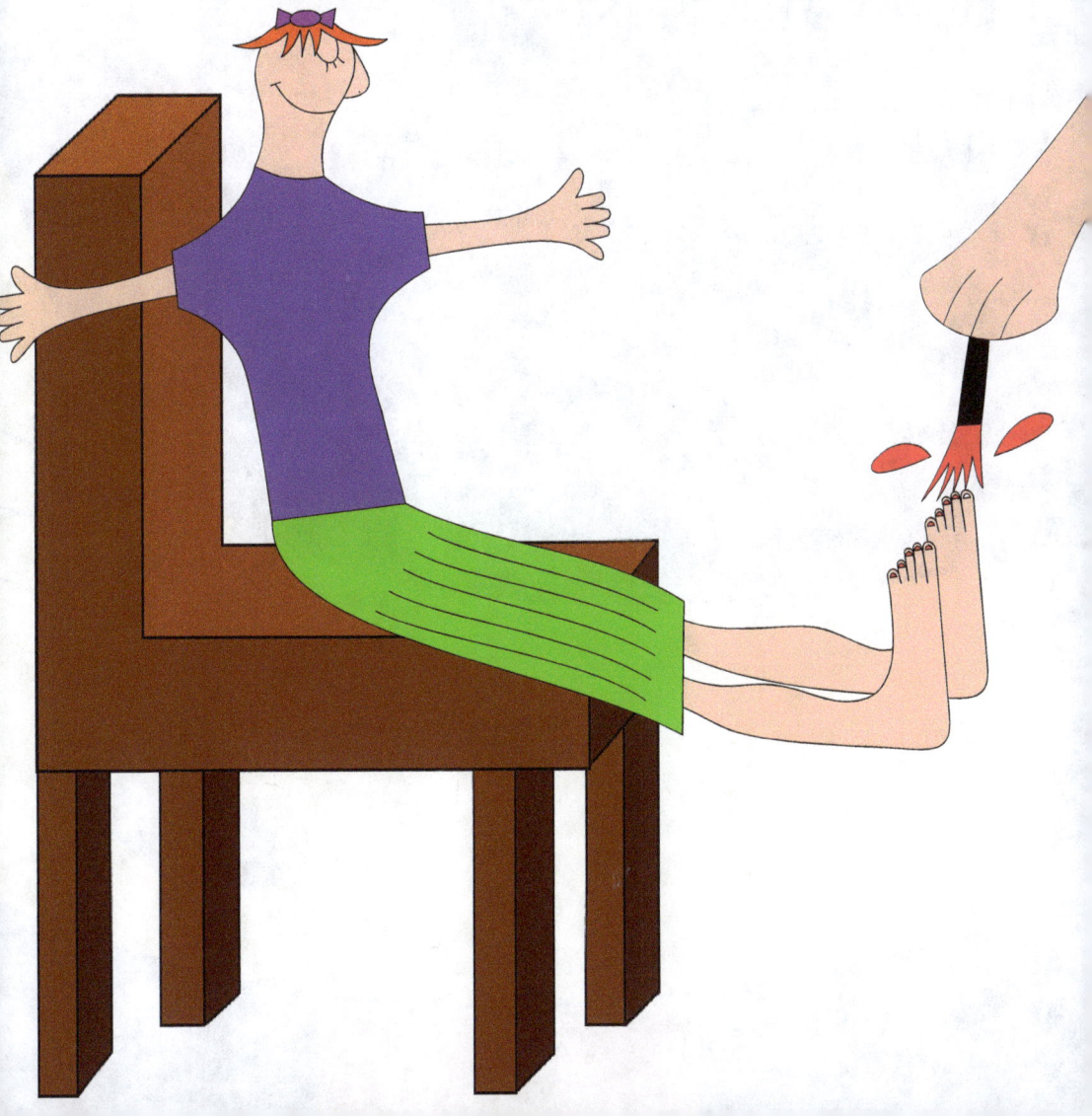

This pretty girl has sliding toes.

The mustelid has climbing toes.

This cheerful boy on the
very high trapeze has
swinging toes.

The happy boy has counting toes.
1, 2, 3, 4, 5! 6, 7, 8, 9, 10!
He has 5 toes on each foot!

The turtle has walking toes in the desert.

The cheetah has running toes in the African grassland.

The lazy boy has tired toes as he walks slowly on the rug.

The bald eagle has grasping toes when he grasps the salmon above the river!

The pig has dirty toes when he has fun in the mud!

The clever girl has clean toes as she washes her feet with a soap and sponge!

The happy boy has tapping toes when he taps his shoes on the dance floor.

The monkey has holding toes when he holds his bananas with his feet.

There are a bunch of BIG bananas on banana trees!

The jumping girl has bouncing toes when she jumps on her trampoline!

The glad boy has snapping toes when he snaps the toes on his feet!

The excited mustelid watches the gecko with crawling toes up on a wall!

How many feet will the gecko's toes crawl up the wall?

The platypus has swimming toes going underwater in the river!

Here come the bubbles right out of his mouth! The mustelid has swimming toes!

The Mustelid Toed Guy has relaxing toes taking his bath and he relaxes!

Everyone does tricks with their toes! What can you do?

Printed in the USA
CPSIA information can be obtained
at www.ICGtesting.com
LVHW010057191023
761274LV00002B/13